Part One

THE OFFICIAL MTO DRIVER'S HANDBOOK

Introduction

Ontario remains a road safety leader in Canada and North America, according to the most recent fatality rate statistics (2008). The Ministry of Transportation has introduced a range of measures to maintain this record and to improve the behaviour of all drivers.

Many collisions are caused by driver error or behaviours such as following too closely, speeding, failure to yield the right of way, improper turns, running red lights and frequently changing lanes. There are also drivers who intentionally put others at risk through such reckless behaviour. Statistics show that new drivers of all ages are far more likely than experienced drivers to be involved in serious or fatal collisions.

Provincial campaigns promoting the correct use of seatbelts and child car seats, and informing people about drinking and driving and aggressive driving, are making a difference. Ontario's Graduated Licensing System (GLS), which lets new drivers gain skills and experience in low-risk environments, is also helping to develop better, safer drivers. Despite the success of GLS, however, statistics show that new drivers of all ages are far more likely than experienced drivers to be involved in serious or fatal collisions.

This handbook gives new drivers the basic information they need about learning to drive in Ontario: the rules of the road, safe driving practices and how to get a licence to drive a car, van or small truck. The ministry recommends that all drivers would benefit from taking an advanced course in driver training.

As you read, remember that this handbook is only a guide. For official descriptions of the laws, look in the *Highway Traffic Act of Ontario* and its Regulations, available at www.e-laws.gov.on.ca. Information on how to get licences to drive other types of vehicles is available in Part Two of this handbook, the Official Motorcycle Handbook, the Official Truck Handbook, the Official Bus Handbook and the Official Air Brake Handbook.

CONTENTS—Part 1

CONTENTS—Part 1

CONTENTS—Part 1

Chapter 1

GETTING YOUR DRIVER'S LICENCE

This chapter tells you what licence you need to drive in Ontario and how to get it, whether you are a new driver, a visitor or a new resident in Ontario.

If you are applying for your first licence, this chapter explains the graduated licensing system, how to apply for a licence, the tests you will have to pass and the driving privileges you will have at each licence level.

Requirements for driving in Ontario

If you live in Ontario, you must be at least 16 years old and have a valid Ontario driver's licence to drive in this province.

If you are a visitor to Ontario and want to drive while you are here, you must be at least 16 years old and have a valid driver's licence from your own province, state or country. If you are from another country and visiting Ontario for more than three months', you need an International Driver's Permit from your own country. If you are taking up residence, you must get an Ontario driver's licence.

If you are a new resident in Ontario and have a valid driver's licence from another province, state or country, you can use it for 60 days after you move to Ontario. If you become a resident of Ontario, you must get an Ontario driver's licence. Ontario has licence exchange agreements with every Canadian province and territory. Also with Australia, Austria, Belgium, France, Germany, Great Britain, the Isle of Man, Japan, Northern Ireland, Korea, Switzerland and the United States.

Driver's Licence Classification Chart

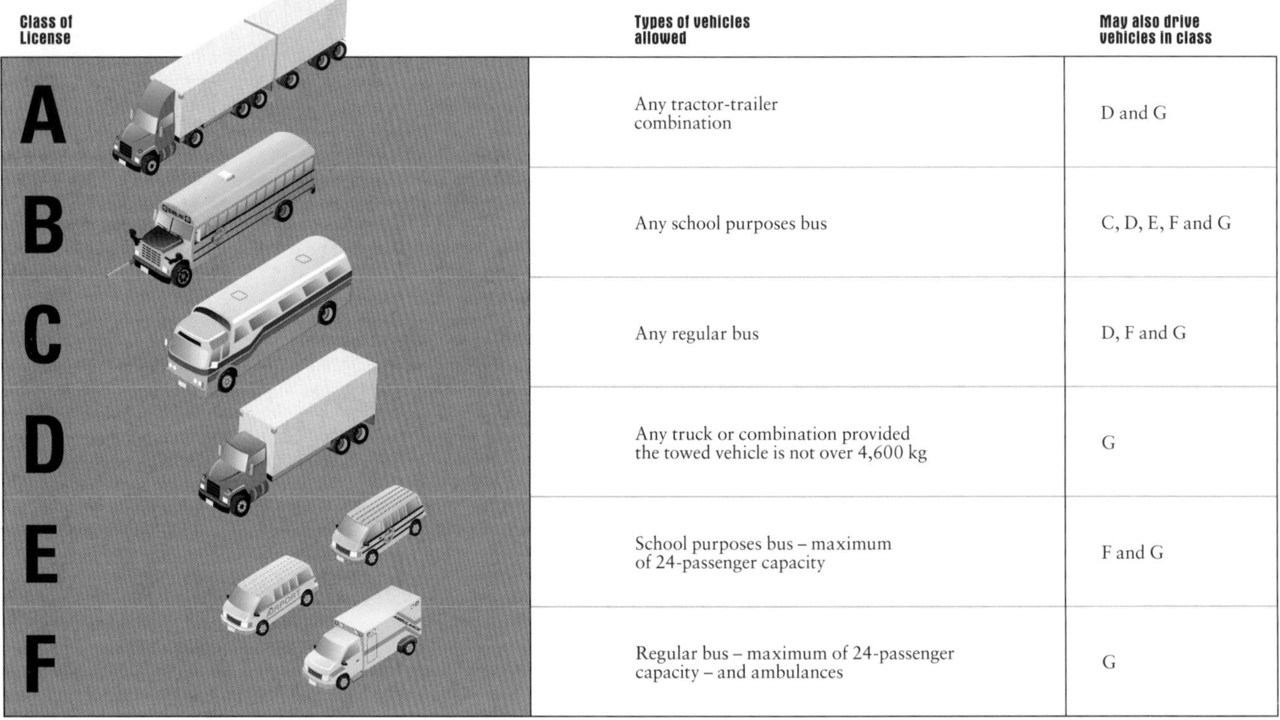

Class of License	Types of vehicles allowed	May also drive vehicles in class
A	Any tractor-trailer combination	D and G
B	Any school purposes bus	C, D, E, F and G
C	Any regular bus	D, F and G
D	Any truck or combination provided the towed vehicle is not over 4,600 kg	G
E	School purposes bus – maximum of 24-passenger capacity	F and G
F	Regular bus – maximum of 24-passenger capacity – and ambulances	G

Diagram 1-1a

Class of License	Types of vehicles allowed
G	Allowed to drive any car, van or small truck or combination of vehicle and towed vehicle up to 11,000 kg provided the towed vehicle is not over 4,600 kg. A pickup truck towing a house trailer exceeds 4,600 kg but the total combined weight of the truck and trailer does not exceed 11,000 kg is deemed a Class G.
G1	Level One of graduated licensing. Holders may drive Class G vehicles with an accompanying fully licensed driver with at least four years' driving experience. Subject to certain conditions.
G2	Level Two of graduated licensing. Holders may drive Class G vehicles without accompanying driver but are subject to certain conditions.
M	Allowed to drive any motorcycles, including motor tricycles, limited-speed motorcycles (motor scooters) and motor-assisted bicycles (mopeds). Holders may also drive a Class G vehicle under the conditions that apply to a Class G1 licence holder.
M1	Level One of graduated licensing for motorcycles, including motor tricycles, limited-speed motorcycles (motor scooters) and motor-assisted bicycles (mopeds). Holders may drive a motorcycle under certain conditions.
M2	Level Two of graduated licensing for motorcycles, including motor tricycles, limited-speed motorcycles (motor scooters) and motor-assisted bicycles (mopeds). Holders may drive a motorcycle but only with a zero blood alcohol level. Holders may also drive a Class G vehicle under the conditions that apply to a Class G1 licence holder.
M with L condition	Holders may operate a limited-speed motorcycle or moped only.
M2 with L condition	Holders may operate a limited-speed motorcycle or moped only.
M with M condition	Holders may operate a motor tricycle only.
M2 with M condition	Holders may operate a motor tricycle only.

Diagram 1-1b

Note: A "Z" air brake endorsement is required on a driver's licence to operate any air brake equipped motor vehicle.

What kind of licence?

In Ontario, there are 14 different kinds of licences. Each one qualifies you to drive a different type of vehicle. The class of licence you have must match the type of vehicle you are driving. You need a Class G licence to drive a car, van or small truck. You must have a Class G licence before you can be licensed to drive any other type of vehicle. The only exception is motorcycles. You may get a motorcycle licence (Class M) without first getting a Class G licence. The Driver's Licence Classification Chart on page 12 to 13 shows you what class of licence you need to drive different vehicles.

For information on the skills and knowledge you'll need to get a Class M motorcycle licence, study the Official Motorcycle Handbook. You can get information on other kinds of licences — classes A, B, C, D, E and F — in the Official Truck Handbook and the Official Bus Handbook. If you want to drive a vehicle equipped with air brakes, the Official Air Brake Handbook tells you how to qualify.

Some recreational vehicles have special licence requirements. If you plan to drive an off-road vehicle or snowmobile, read the Off-Road Vehicles section in this handbook.

You do not need a licence to ride a bicycle in Ontario; however bicycles are defined as vehicles in the Highway Traffic Act and bicyclists have rights and responsibilities similar to other vehicle operators under the Act. Information on safe cycling can be found in the Ministry of Transportation publications *Cycling Skills and the Young Cyclists' Guide.*

Graduated licensing

New drivers applying for their first car or motorcycle licence enter Ontario's graduated licensing system. Graduated licensing lets new drivers get driving experience and skills gradually. The two-step licensing process takes at least 20 months' to complete.

To apply for a licence, you must be at least 16 years old, pass a vision test and pass a test of your knowledge of the rules of the road and traffic signs. After you pass these tests, you will enter Level One and get a Class G1 licence.

You must pass two road tests to become fully licensed. Passing the first road test lets you move to Level Two (Class G2) and the second one gives you full Class G driving privileges.

Applying for a licence

To apply for a licence, you must show proof of your legal name, date of birth (showing day, month and year of birth) and signature. Documents must be original and valid. Photocopies and expired documents are not acceptable.

Any one of the following documents may be used to satisfy the requirement to provide proof of legal name, complete date of birth and signature:

- Passport (Canadian or foreign);
- Canadian Citizenship Card with photo;
- Permanent immigration documents:
  - Permanent Resident Card (PRC); or
  - Record of Landing (Form 1000); or
  - Confirmation of Permanent Residence (Form IMM 5292);
- Temporary immigration documents:
  - Student Authorization (IMM 1442);
  - Employment Authorization (IMM 1442);
  - Visitor Record (IMM 1442);
  - Temporary Resident's Permit (IMM 1442);
  - Refugee Status Claim (IMM 1434);
  - Acknowledgement of Intent to Claim Refugee Status (IMM 7703 with photo);
  - Report Pursuant to the Immigration Act (IMM 1442 with photo).

Additional documents

Additional documents are required if the document presented from the list above does not indicate the legal name, complete date of birth (day, month, year) or signature. The additional documents must provide proof of the missing or incomplete information.

The following documents are acceptable as proof of date of birth and legal name:

- Canadian or U.S. Birth Certificate.

The following documents are acceptable as proof of signature:

- Driver's Licence (Canadian and U.S. only);
- Identity Card with signature (issued by Canadian province/ territory or U.S. state authority);
- Canadian Certificate of Indian Status;
- Ontario Student Card with signature;
- Ontario Health Card with applicant's signature. (Clients may choose to produce their Ontario Health Card for proof of signature. The Health Card and Health Number will not be recorded or photocopied.)

Proof of legal name

If additional documents presented to prove date of birth or signature do not indicate the applicant's legal name (i.e. name has been changed or is different on the two documents presented), the applicant will be required to provide additional documents as proof of legal name. The following additional documents are acceptable as proof of legal name:

- Marriage Certificate (Canadian or Foreign, government issued);
- Change of Name Certificate;
- Court Order for adoption, change of name or divorce (must bear

legal name, date of birth and court seal).

To confirm complete date of birth where no or only partial date of birth is available:

- Sworn affidavit stating reason why partial or no date is available, with supporting documents. Please contact the Ministry of Transportation's Driver and Vehicle Licensing Call Centre at (416) 235-2999 or toll free at 1-800-387-3445 (Canada-wide) for further information.

Note: Direct identification by a parent or guardian is not acceptable. The applicant is required to present an acceptable document with his or her own signature.

Declaration from a Guarantor

If an applicant is unable to present one of the above documents as proof of signature, the applicant may present an original, completed Declaration from a Guarantor form attesting to their signature. Applicants must first ensure that no other acceptable documents for signature are available from the list identified above. To obtain a Guarantor form:

- download the Declaration from a Guarantor form from the Ministry of Transportation's website at www.mto.gov.on.ca or the DriveTest website at www.drivetest.ca; or,
- request a copy of the form at any DriveTest Centre.

Bring the documents to a DriveTest Centre or Travel Point (a temporary DriveTest Centre where there is no regional centre). Phone ahead to find out where the nearest Travel Point is and when it is open. You will find the telephone number under "Drivers and Vehicles" in the Government of Ontario section of the blue pages in your phone book. You can also find it on the Internet at www.drivetest.ca.

You must pay a fee when you apply. This fee includes the cost of the knowledge test, your first road test and a five-year licensing fee. There are more charges for your second road test and for any retests you may need to take. In order to schedule a road test appointment, you must prepay the road test fee.

When you apply for your licence, you will be asked questions about your health. People with certain physical or medical conditions are not allowed to drive for safety reasons. If your physical or medical condition means you cannot be licensed, you will be told when you apply.

Once you have a licence, you should report any change in your medical condition that may affect your ability to drive safely. By law, doctors and optometrists must report the name and address of anyone over 16 who has a condition that may make it unsafe for him or her to drive.

For further details on applying for a licence visit the Ministry of Transportation's website at www.mto.gov.on.ca.

Graduated licensing requirements

Here are the rules you must follow at each level:

Level One (Class G1):

Level One lasts 12 months'.
The Ministry of Transportation encourages all new drivers to take an approved driver education course to help learn the proper driving skills and knowledge. You should begin your training as soon as you become a Level One driver so you can get as much driving experience as possible. If you pass an approved course, you can complete Level One in eight months'. While at Level One, the following rules apply:

- You must not drive if you have been drinking alcohol. Your blood alcohol level must be zero.
- You must not drive alone; an accompanying driver must sit in the front passenger seat. This is the only person who can be in the front seat with you while you drive. The accompanying driver must have a valid Class G (or higher) licence, at least four years of driving experience, and must have a blood alcohol level of less than .05 per cent when accompanying you. Time spent at the Class G2 level, as long as the G2 licence was valid (not suspended), does count toward the accompanying driver's four years of experience. The accompanying driver's licence may have demerit points, but it cannot be suspended.
- Each person in the vehicle must have a working seatbelt.
- You must not drive on 400-series highways with a posted speed limit over 80km/h. Also you must not drive on certain high-speed roads including the Queen Elizabeth Way, Don Valley Parkway and the Gardiner Expressway in the Greater Toronto Area, the E.C. Row Expressway in Windsor and the Conestoga Parkway in Kitchener-Waterloo. However, if your accompanying driver is a driving instructor, you may drive on any road.
- You must not drive between midnight and 5:00 a.m.

You must pass a road test of your driving skills to move to Level Two. At this time, you will be given a Class G2 licence.

G1 knowledge test – checklist

Before taking the G1 knowledge test, make sure you have studied the Official Driver's Handbook.

Bring the following items to the test:

- 2 pieces of identification;
- Money for test fees – cash, debit or credit card;

- Glasses or contact lenses (if you need to wear them to drive).

G1 exit test – checklist

Before taking the G1 exit test, make sure you have studied the Official Driver's Handbook.

Bring the following items to the test:

- Vehicle in good working order (see page 20);
- Money for test fees (if applicable);
- Glasses or contact lenses (if you need to wear them to drive);
- Beginner Driver Education Student Record (if licensed between 8 and 12 months');
- Arrive at least 30 minutes before Road Test appointment.

Level Two (Class G2):

Level Two lasts at least 12 months'. At this level, you have more privileges because of your driving experience. At Level Two:

- You must not drive if you have been drinking alcohol. Your blood alcohol level must be zero.
- Each person in the vehicle must have a working seatbelt.

In addition, the following restrictions apply between the hours of midnight and 5 a.m. to G2 drivers aged 19 years and under.

- In the first six months' after receiving your G2 licence, you are allowed to carry only one passenger aged 19 or under.
- After six months' with your G2 licence and until you obtain your full G licence or turn 20, you are allowed to carry up to three passengers aged 19 or under.

Exemptions: The passenger restrictions for G2 drivers aged 19 and under do not apply if you are accompanied by a fully-licensed driver in the front passenger seat, or if the passengers are members of your immediate family (a guardian, or those related to you by blood, marriage, common-law relationship, or adoption).

After 12 months' at Level Two, you may take a road test to qualify for full licence privileges. You must pass this test to get a Class G licence.

Note: It is now law that all young drivers 21 and under, regardless of licence class, must have a blood alcohol level of zero.

Note: A restricted Class M licence for limited-speed motorcycle and moped drivers allows licence holders to drive only a limited-speed motorcycle and moped. You are not permitted to drive a limited-speed motorcycle or moped on any driver's licence other than a class M licence (including M1, M2(L), M2, M(L) or M). For more information on how to obtain a restricted Class M licence to drive a moped, and graduated licensing requirements, please read the Official Motorcycle Handbook.

Road tests

Road tests check your driving skills in the vehicle and in traffic. You will be tested on your ability to follow the rules of the road and safe driving practices.

The Level One road test deals with basic driving skills. The Level Two road test deals with more advanced knowledge and driving skills. Your performance in each of the tests will tell you whether you need more training or practice.

When you feel qualified to drive safely and confident enough to take your road test, contact the Road Test Booking Call Centre at (416) 325-8580 or 1-888-570-6110, or go online to www.mto.gov.on.ca, to schedule an appointment. If you are unable to keep the appointment, call the Road Test Booking Call Centre or go online to cancel your test. If you fail to attend or you cancel your appointment without providing at least 48 hours notice, your prepaid road test fee will not be refunded.

You must bring the appropriate vehicle to each of your road tests. Make sure it is in good working order and you feel comfortable driving it. Bring your current licence to the appointment. If you are a Level One driver, an accompanying driver must come with you to the test centre. (See description of accompanying driver in Level One (Class G1) on page 17.) If you are a Level Two driver, please be prepared to take alternate transportation home in case you fail your road test and are unqualified to drive.

No pets or passengers other than the driver examiner are allowed in the vehicle during a road test.

All road tests have a set time frame. Before you begin your test, the examiner will inform you of the amount of time you have to complete the test. You will not be asked to do anything illegal during the road test. The examiner will explain the test and you should follow her or his instructions. The examiner is not allowed to coach you during the test, so if you have any questions, ask them before you begin.

While the Level One road test checks your basic driving skills, the Level Two road test is much more demanding. You should learn the proper driving skills as soon as you become a Level One driver so you can get as much driving experience as possible before taking the Level Two test.

For the Level Two test, you must demonstrate a high level of driving skill and knowledge. You will also have to show that you can drive well on a freeway or high speed highway.

While you are taking the test, the examiner will be watching to see how well you control your vehicle and perform such driving tasks as starting, stopping, turning, parallel parking and three-point turning. The examiner will check your observation skills, including when and how often you use the mirrors, where you look, and how you respond to traffic, signs, pavement markings and possible hazards.

You will be tested on how well you manage the space around your vehicle, your ability to make safe lane changes and how closely you follow and stop behind other vehicles. How you communicate with other road users, using turn signals and brake lights and making eye contact with other drivers and pedestrians, will also be noted, as well as the correctness of your driving decisions, such as knowing when to yield the right-of-way. For more information on the Level Two road test, see Chapter 6.

At the end of each test, the examiner will give you a complete report of your skills and explain any mistakes you have made. If you fail the test, the report will show you where you need to improve. When you have had more practice, you can make an appointment to take the test again. You must wait at least 10 days between tests.

G2 exit test – checklist

You must have highway driving experience (experience driving on highways with speed limits of at least 80 km/h) before taking the G2 exit test. You must complete a Declaration of Highway Driving Experience form, describing the highway driving experience you have, before taking the road test. Bring the following items to the test:

- Vehicle in good working order (see Out-of-Order road test on this page);
- Money for test fees (if applicable);
- Glasses or contact lenses (if you need to wear them to drive);
- Arrive at least 30 minutes before Road Test appointment.

Failure to attend road test, or short notice cancellation

If you cancel or reschedule your road test appointment with less than 48 hours notice, or if you fail to attend your appointment, your prepaid road test fee will not be refunded. Under certain extenuating circumstances only (such as a death in your immediate family), the road test fee will remain as a credit on your driving record.

Out-of-order road test

If your vehicle does not meet ministry standards for the purpose of a road test, or if there is a non-vehicle related reason for which the examiner determines that the road test cannot be completed, the examiner declares the road test out-of-order. If your road test is declared out-of-order, you lose 50% of your road test fee. The other 50% of the fee remains as a credit on your driving record, and may be applied when booking a new road test. In order to book the new road test, you will have to pay the 50% of the fee deducted due to the out-of-order.

If you have any concerns that your road test may be declared out-of-order, contact the DriveTest Centre before your scheduled test to discuss it.

New Ontario residents

If you are a new resident of Ontario and have a valid driver's licence from another province or country, you can use that licence for 60 days in Ontario. If you want to continue to drive after 60 days, you must get an Ontario driver's licence.

Effective May 1, 2006, licensed driving experience for out-of-country applicants will be credited as follows

Requirements for all driver's licence applicants

- All applicants for an Ontario driver's licence are required to present a valid foreign driver's licence (if it is not in English or French, it is to be accompanied by a written translation from a qualified translator), pass a vision test and a written knowledge test regarding Ontario's traffic rules, pay all applicable fees, and provide acceptable proof of identity.
- Applicants who fulfill these requirements can obtain a G1 licence.
- All applicants must declare their licensed driving experience on the driver's licence application form.
- Applicants are required to provide adequate proof of foreign licensed driving experience. However, if that is not possible, the ministry will accept an applicant's declaration of their foreign licensed driving experience on the driver's licence application for up to a maximum of 12 months' licensed experience.
- This policy only applies to applicants for Class G licences.

Applicants declaring less than 12 months' licensed driving experience within the preceding three years

- Applicants are credited with the amount of licensed driving experience declared on the driver's licence application.
- Applicants must have 12 months' licensed driving experience before attempting the G1 road test.
- If an applicant successfully completes a ministry-approved Beginner Driver Education course, the mandatory waiting time, prior to taking the G1 road test, will be reduced from 12 to 8 months'.
- The 8-12 months' may be a combination of licensed driving experience in the foreign jurisdiction and licensed experience in Ontario.

Applicants declaring more than 12 months' licensed driving experience but less than 24 months' within the preceding three years:

- Applicants will be credited with 12 months' licensed driving experience and may proceed to take the G1 road test without having to fulfill the mandatory 12-month G1 wait period.
- If the applicant passes the G1 road test, they will be issued a G2 licence and will not be subject to the six restrictions of the G1 licence, including the requirement to have a fully licensed driver accompany them in the vehicle and prohibition from driving on 400-series expressways.
- To obtain credit for more than 12 months' licensed driving experience, applicants are required to obtain written authentication of their foreign licensed driving experience from the originating licensing agency, or from the Embassy, Consulate or High Commissioners' offices representing the jurisdiction. The authentication letter must be on official letterhead and be written in either English or French.
- Applicants will be credited with their foreign licensed driving experience as certified on the authentication letter.
- Credited licensed driving experience will be applied toward the G2 12-month waiting period prior to taking the G2 road test.
- If applicants do not provide a letter of authentication, applicants must fulfill the 12-month mandatory waiting period prior to taking the G2 road test.

Applicants declaring a minimum of 24 months' licensed driving experience within the preceding three years:

- To obtain credit for more than 12 months' licensed driving experience, applicants are required to obtain written authentication of their foreign licensed driving experience from the originating licensing agency, or from the Embassy, Consulate or High Commissioners' offices representing the jurisdiction. The authentication letter must be on official letterhead and be written in either English or French.
- Applicants will be credited with their foreign licensed driving experience as certified on the authentication letter.
- Applicants have, pending a letter of authentication of a minimum of 24 months' of foreign licensed driving experience, the option of attempting the G1 or G2 exit road tests (mandatory waiting times are waived).
- If the applicant chooses to attempt the G1 road test and successfully completes it, the applicant will

then be eligible to attempt the G2 road test.
- Upon successfully passing the G2 exit road test, applicants will be issued a G licence.
- If applicants do not provide a letter of authentication, applicants must pass the G1 road test and must fulfill the 12-month waiting period prior to taking the G2 road test.

Who does the policy affect?

The policy applies to all applicants coming from either a foreign jurisdiction that does not have a driver's licence reciprocal agreement with Ontario, or a U.S. state that is not part of the Inter-provincial Record Exchange.

This policy does not apply to drivers from the following jurisdictions:

- Canadian provinces and territories;
- Canadian Forces Europe;
- U.S. states;
- Australia, Austria, Belgium, France, Great Britain, Germany, Isle of Man, Japan, Korea and Switzerland.

Motorcycle licence exchanges

Exchange agreements apply to licensed motorcycle drivers from Canada, the United States, Australia and Switzerland. If you have less than two years of driving experience, you may get credit for your experience and enter Level Two of the graduated licensing system. Once you have a total of two years of driving experience, you may take the Level Two road test to earn full driving privileges.

There is no exchange agreement for motorcycle drivers from Austria, Belgium, France, Germany, Great Britain, the Isle of Man, Japan and Korea. However, credit for holding a motorcycle licence from one of these countries will be granted for previous motorcycle experience when applying for a Class M motorcycle licence in Ontario.

If you hold a motorcycle licence from another Canadian jurisdiction that is equivalent to Ontario's restricted Class M licence, you will be able to exchange your licence for a restricted Class M Ontario licence.

Driving customs vary from place to place. That is why experienced drivers from other countries should familiarize themselves with Ontario's laws. The Official Driver's Handbook and the Ministry of Transportation website are good resources.

COULD YOU PASS?

The rest of this handbook gives you information you need to pass your tests and to keep your driving privileges once you get your licence. The written test may ask you about:

- seatbelts;
- traffic signs and lights;
- emergency vehicles;
- how to use headlights;
- speed limits;
- getting on or off a freeway;
- what drivers must do when they meet streetcars and school buses;
- driver licence suspensions;
- the demerit point system;
- passing other vehicles;
- collision reporting;
- sharing the road with other road users;
- rules of the road.

The road tests will test how well you use your knowledge while driving. You will be tested on:

- starting, stopping and turning;
- traffic signs and lights;
- passing vehicles, including bicycles, and driving in passing lanes;
- travelling through controlled and uncontrolled intersections;
- parallel parking and reversing;
- foreseeing hazardous conditions and being ready for them;
- other safe driving practices.

Make sure you know the information in this handbook before you take these tests. To see sample test questions that could appear on the knowledge test, see page 153.

Chapter 1 — Summary

By the end of this chapter you should know:

- The legal requirements you must meet to obtain a driver's licence;
- The different licence classifications and what type of vehicle they permit you to drive;
- The identification you need to provide when applying for a driver's licence;
- The restrictions and testing requirements under the graduated licensing system.

Chapter 2

SAFE AND RESPONSIBLE DRIVING

Being a safe and responsible driver takes a combination of knowledge, skill and attitude.

To begin, you must know the traffic laws and driving practices that help traffic move safely. Breaking these "rules of the road" is the major cause of collisions.

Traffic laws are made by federal, provincial and municipal governments, and police from each level can enforce them. If you break a traffic law, you may be fined, sent to jail or lose your driver's licence. If you get caught driving while your licence is suspended your vehicle may be impounded.

But you need to do more than just obey the rules. You must care about the safety of others on the road. Everyone is responsible for avoiding collisions. Even if someone else does something wrong, you may be found responsible for a collision if you could have done something to avoid it.

Because drivers have to cooperate to keep traffic moving safely, you must also be predictable, doing what other people using the road expect you to do. And you must be courteous. Courteous driving means giving other drivers space to change lanes, not cutting them off and signalling your turns and lane changes properly.

You must be able to see dangerous situations before they happen and to respond quickly and effectively to prevent them. This is called defensive or strategic driving. There are collision avoidance courses available where you can practice these techniques.

Defensive driving is based on three ideas: visibility, space and communication.

Visibility is about seeing and being seen. You should always be aware of traffic in front, behind and beside you. Keep your eyes constantly moving, scanning the road ahead and

to the side and checking your mirrors every five seconds or so. The farther ahead you look, the less likely you will be surprised, and you will have time to avoid any hazards. Make sure other drivers can see you by using your signal lights as required.

Managing the **space** around your vehicle lets you see and be seen and gives you time and space to avoid a collision. Leave a cushion of space ahead, behind and to both sides. Because the greatest risk of a collision is in front of you, stay well back.

Communicate with other road users to make sure they see you and know what you are doing. Make eye contact with pedestrians, cyclists and drivers at intersections and signal whenever you want to slow down, stop, turn or change lanes. If you need to get another person's attention, use your horn.

I. Getting ready to drive

Before you drive, make sure you are comfortable with your physical, mental, and emotional state, your vehicle and the conditions in which you will be driving. If you have doubts about any of them, don't drive.

Your ability to drive can change from one day to the next. Illness, fatigue, prescription and over-the-counter drugs, stress and your mental or emotional state can greatly diminish your ability to operate a motor vehicle. You should consider these factors before you begin driving, and you should not operate a motor vehicle when you are not fit to do so.

Be physically and mentally alert

You must be in good physical and mental condition to drive. Don't drive when you are sick or injured or when you have been drinking alcohol or taking any drug or medication that may reduce your ability to drive.

Don't drive when you are tired. You might fall asleep at the wheel, risking the lives of others on the road. Even if you don't fall asleep, fatigue affects your driving ability. Your thinking slows down and you miss seeing things. In an emergency, you may make the wrong decision or you may not make the right decision fast enough.

Don't drive when you are upset or angry. Strong emotions can reduce your ability to think and react quickly.

Know your vehicle

Get to know your vehicle before you drive it. There are many types of vehicles available today with many different characteristics, including fuel ignition systems, anti-lock brakes, 4-wheel drive, and systems for traction control and stability control. Check the vehicle owner's manual. For driving in difficult situations and conditions see the section on dealing with particular situations on page 71.

Make sure you know where all the controls and instruments are and

Diagram 2-1

what they do. Check that all warning lights and gauges work. Watch for a warning light that stays on after you drive away; it could mean a serious problem with your vehicle.

Get to know the controls well enough to turn on wipers and washers, headlights, highbeams, heater and defroster without having to look. Learning to use these essential controls without taking your eyes off the road is an important part of driving.

Get into position

Make sure you sit properly behind the wheel. You should sit high enough in the driver's seat to see over the steering wheel and hood. You should be able to see the ground four metres in front of the vehicle. Use a firm cushion if needed.

Be sure that you are sitting straight upright in the seat with your elbows slightly bent. Adjust the seat so your feet reach the pedals easily. To check your position, try placing your feet flat on the floor under the brake pedal. If you can do this without stretching, you are seated properly. This keeps you in the proper, upright sitting position and gives you more stability when manoeuvring your vehicle.

If your vehicle has an adjustable headrest, you should make sure it is at the right height. The back of your head should be directly in front of the middle of the headrest to protect you in a collision.

Check that you have enough room in the front seat to drive properly and safely. Do not overcrowd your driving space with passengers or property.

Diagram 2-2

Keep a clear view

Keep a clear view when driving. Do not put anything in your windows that will block your view. The windows of your vehicle must not be coated with any material that keeps you from seeing out in any direction. Neither should the windshield or front door windows be coated to keep someone from seeing inside the vehicle.

Find your blind spots

Check and adjust your mirrors and find your blind spots, the area on each

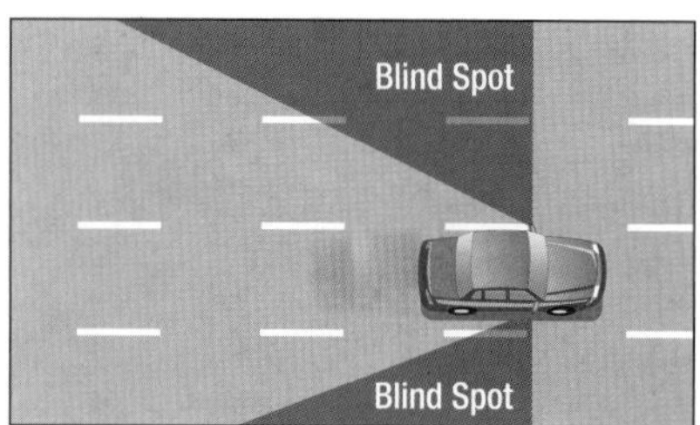

Diagram 2-3

side of your vehicle where you cannot see. You may not see people or cyclists when they are in these spots. On some vehicles the blind spot is so large that a vehicle could be there and you would not see it.

Adjust your mirrors so that there are as few blind spots as possible. Blind spots in most vehicles are to the back left and back right of the vehicle. To reduce the blind spots even more, position the interior mirror so that the centre of the mirror shows the centre of the rear window. You should be able to see directly behind the car when the interior mirror is properly adjusted. Position the left outside mirror by leaning towards the window and moving the mirror so that you can just see the rear of your car. Position the right outside mirror by leaning to the centre of the vehicle and moving the mirror so that you can again just see the rear of your car. Avoid overlap in what you can see in your mirrors. Because your side mirrors show only narrow angles of view, turning your head to do shoulder checks is the only way to make sure there is nothing in your blind spots.

You should know the blind spots on your own vehicle. You can learn where and how large they are by having someone walk around your car and watching the person in the mirrors.

Fasten your seatbelt

The proper use of a seatbelt can save your life. Even a small increase in the number of people that wear their seatbelts can save many lives.

You must use your seatbelt every time you travel in any vehicle equipped with seatbelts. All passengers must be buckled up in their own seatbelt, child car seat or booster seat.

Drivers who do not buckle up can be fined up to $1000 and will be given two demerit points. Drivers may also be fined and receive demerit points if they fail to ensure that all passengers under 16 years of age are properly buckled in a seatbelt, child car seat or booster seat. Level One (G1) drivers are only allowed to have his or her accompanying driver as a passenger, and must have a seatbelt for him or her. Novice drivers must have a seatbelt for every passenger. Drivers who do not ensure there is a working seatbelt for every passenger can lose their licence for at least 30 days.

Seatbelts should be worn snugly enough to keep you in your seat during a collision. Never put more than one person into a seatbelt; this

Diagram 2-4

can cause serious injury or even death in a collision. Wear the shoulder strap over your shoulder, never under your arm or behind your back. The lap belt should be worn low over the hips, not against the stomach.

Use your seatbelt always, even when you are sitting in a position with an active airbag. Airbags do not replace seatbelts. In a collision, your seatbelt will keep you in position so that the airbag can protect you.

Note: The safest place a passenger can travel is inside a vehicle, properly buckled in. It is not safe to travel outside a vehicle, such as in the back of a pickup truck, or in a trailer that is being towed. It is important for passengers to be secured within a vehicle to avoid being thrown from the vehicle during a collision.

For more information on seatbelts visit www.ontario.ca/transportation or call ServiceOntario Transportation Info Line (416) 235-4686 (1-800-268-4686).

Child safety

To be safely protected in a vehicle, children must be properly secured in a child car seat, booster seat or seatbelt, depending on their height, weight and/or age. Research shows that a correctly used child car seat can reduce the likelihood of injury or death by 75 percent.

As a driver, you are responsible for ensuring that all passengers under 16 years of age are properly buckled into a seatbelt, child car seat or booster seat. The fine for not us-

Diagram 2-5

ing a child car seat or booster seat as required by law is up to $1,000 plus two demerit points on conviction. In Ontario, all drivers are required to use proper child car seats and booster seats when transporting young children.

Child car seats must meet Canadian Motor Vehicle Safety Standards (CMVSS). Buckles and straps must be fastened according to the manufacturer's instructions. Newer vehicles that come equipped with a lower Universal Anchorage System (UAS) for securing a child car seat, do not require the use of a seatbelt. A booster seat requires a lap and shoulder belt combination.

Infants who weigh less than 9 kg (20 lbs.) must be buckled into a rear-facing child car seat attached to the vehicle by a seatbelt or the UAS strap. A rear-facing child car seat is always best installed in the back seat. Never put a rear-facing child car seat in a seating position that has an active airbag. If the airbag inflates, it could seriously injure the child.

Toddlers 9 to 18 kg (20 to 40 lbs.) must be buckled into a child car seat attached to the vehicle by a seatbelt or a UAS strap; the seat's tether strap must also be attached to the vehicle's tether anchor. Children weighing beyond 9 kg (20 lbs) may remain in a rear-facing child car seat if the car seat is designed to accommodate the child's height and weight. Always follow the manufacturer's instructions when installing a child car seat in your vehicle.

Booster seats provide 60 percent more protection than seatbelts alone. These must be used by pre-school and primary grade-aged children who have outgrown their forward-facing childcar seat, are under the age of eight and weigh 18 kg (40 lbs.) or more but less than 36 kg (80 lbs.), and who are less than 145 cm (4 feet, 9 inches) tall. Booster seats raise a child up so that the adult seatbelt works more effectively. The child's head must be supported by the top of the booster, vehicle seat or headrest. You must use a booster seat with a lap/shoulder belt. The lap/shoulder belt should be worn so that the shoulder belt fits closely against the body, over the shoulder and across the center of the chest and the lap belt sits firmly against the body and across the hips. Always follow the manufacturer's instructions when installing a booster seat in your vehicle, and secure the booster seat with a seatbelt when a child is not traveling in it, or remove it from the vehicle.

If your vehicle has lap belts only, secure the child by the lap belt only. Never use a lap belt alone with a booster seat.

Children may begin wearing a seatbelt once they are able to wear it properly (a lap belt flat across the hips, shoulder belt across the centre of the chest and over the shoulder), and if any one of the following criteria is met:

- the child turns eight years old;
- the child weighs 36 kg (80 lbs) or more; or,
- the child is 145 cm (4 feet 9 inches) tall or taller.

Do not place a child in a seating position in front of an air bag that is not turned off. The safest place for a child under age 13 is in the back seat.

Always secure loose objects in the vehicle with cargo nets or straps, or move them to the trunk to prevent them from injuring passengers in a collision or sudden stop.

Correct installation of a child car seat is important for ensuring a child's safety. Your local public health unit is a good resource for finding out how to properly install a child car seat, or visit a local car seat clinic where certified technicians will help you install the seat.

For more information on child car seats visit www.ontario.ca/transportation for important tips and installation videos or call ServiceOntario Transportation Info at (416) 235-4686 (1-800-268-4686).

Note: Be careful if buying a used child car seat. Considerations should include ensuring the child car seat comes with complete manufacturer's instructions and all necessary equipment; does not show signs of deterioration or damage; has never been in a collision; is not under recall; and has not exceeded its useful life expectancy as determined by the manufacturer.

Seatbelts and child car seats save lives

Seatbelts and child car seats reduce the risk of injury or death in collisions.

- Seatbelts help keep you inside and in control of the vehicle during a collision. People who are thrown from a vehicle have a much lower chance of surviving a collision.
- Seatbelts keep your head and body from hitting the inside of the vehicle or another person in the vehicle. When a vehicle hits a solid object, the people inside keep moving until something stops them. If you are not wearing your seatbelt, the steering wheel, windshield, dashboard or another person might be what stops you. This "human collision" often causes serious injury.
- Fire or sinking in water is rare in collisions. If it does happen, seatbelts help keep you conscious, giving you a chance to get out of the vehicle.
- In a sudden stop or swerve, no one can hold onto a child who is not in a seatbelt or child car seat. Infants or children who are not properly restrained can be thrown against the vehicle's interior, collide with other people or be ejected.
- When using a child car seat, make sure that the seat is tightly secured by the vehicle seatbelt or by the Universal Anchorage System (UAS) strap, and for a forward-facing car seat, ensure the tether strap is also used. When installing the child car seat, press one knee into the seat and use your body weight to push it into the vehicle seat, then tighten the seatbelt or the car seat UAS strap as much as possible. The installed child car seat should move no more than 2.5 cm (1 inch) where the seatbelt or

UAS strap is routed through the child car seat.

- Use a locking clip where needed to ensure the seatbelt stays locked into position and will not loosen during a collision. Refer to your vehicle owner's manual to see if you will need to use a locking clip.
- If a rear-facing child car seat does not rest at the proper 45-degree angle, you can prop up the base of the seat with a towel or a Styrofoam bar ("pool noodle"). Eighty per cent of the base of a forward-facing car seat should be firmly supported by the vehicle seat.

Turn on headlights at night and in poor conditions

Headlights enable you to see the roadway in front of your vehicle when visibility is poor, as well as making your vehicle visible to others. Your vehicle's headlights must shine a white light that can be seen at least 150 metres in front and is strong enough to light up objects 110 metres away. You must also have red rear lights that can be seen 150 metres away and a white light lighting the rear licence plate when headlights are on. Headlights are equipped with the option to use a highbeam to enhance vision further down the roadway and the use of a lowbeam when you are near other vehicles to minimize the glare of your headlights onto others. When you use highbeam headlights, remember to switch to lowbeams within 150 metres of an oncoming vehicle. Use your lowbeams when you are less than 60 metres behind another vehicle unless you are passing it. These rules apply to all roads, including divided ones.

Diagram 2-6: Highbeams

Diagram 2-7: Lowbeams

Turning your headlights on activates other required light systems, such as your parking lights, tail lights, and rear licence plate light.

Daytime running lights, which are often another mode of your headlights or can be a separate lighting system, are specifically designed to make your vehicle more visible during times of good light conditions, and are automatically activated when your vehicle is in operation and your headlight switch is turned to off.

When driving your vehicle, headlights are required to be turned on between one-half hour before sunset and one-half hour after sunrise, and any other time of poor light conditions, such as fog, snow or rain, which keeps you from clearly seeing people or vehicles less than 150 metres away. Please see the section on driving at night and in bad weather. Don't drive with only one headlight or with lights that are not aimed properly. Have your full lighting system checked regularly, keep them clean, and replace burned-out bulbs as soon as possible.

Your daytime running lights are not to be used as headlights during poor lighting conditions. They provide an inappropriate form of light that may cast glare onto others or deactivate other required light systems, such as tail lights. Daytime running lights are only to be used during good light conditions to enhance the visibility of your vehicle. If your vehicle is not equipped with daytime running lights, you should turn your headlights on to provide similar visual enhancement.

Driving with your vehicle's full lighting system set to automatic is recommended, if your vehicle is equipped with this option. This will better ensure that the appropriate lighting system is being used. You should also monitor the activation and operation of your vehicle's full lighting system at all times to ensure that appropriate lighting is being provided.

Chapter 2, section I — Summary

By the end of this section you should know:

- The concepts of safe and responsible and defensive driving
- Factors that may affect your physical and mental readiness to drive
- How to familiarize yourself with your vehicle's controls and how to set your seating position
- The legal requirements surrounding seatbelts, booster seats, and child car seats
- How and when to use your vehicle's lighting system

II. Driving along

Always be aware of traffic around you as you drive. Develop a routine for looking ahead, behind and from side to side. Check your mirrors every five seconds or so, and check your blind spots by turning your head to look over your shoulder. Keep other drivers out of your blind spot by changing your speed and don't drive in other vehicles' blind spots. This is especially true when driving around large commercial vehicles as they typically have large blind spots to the sides and back. Be extra careful at dusk and dawn when everyone has difficulty adjusting to the changing light.

Keep a cushion of space around your vehicle and be prepared for the unexpected. Anticipate other drivers movements and make allowances for every possible error. Look well ahead and watch for people in parked vehicles, they may be about to pull out in front of you or to open a door.

Diagram 2-8

Watch for smaller vehicles, bicycles and pedestrians.

Steer smoothly

All steering should be smooth and precise. You should do most steering and lane changes without taking either hand off the wheel. You must be able to steer in a straight line while shifting gears, adjusting controls or checking your blind spot.

Picture the steering wheel as a clock and place your hands at nine o'clock and three o'clock.

Use of turn signals and brake lights

Signals tell other drivers what you want to do, alerting them to your intention to turn or stop.

Use your turn signals and brake lights to signal before stopping, slowing down, turning, changing lanes, leaving the road or moving out from a parked position. Give the correct signal well before taking the action and make sure other drivers can see it. Check that the way is clear before you act, just signalling is not enough. Follow the rules for turns, whether left or right, on lane changes and on yields to other vehicles and pedestrians.

If your turn signals and brake lights are not working, use hand and arm signals. The pictures on this page show how to make hand and arm signals. When watching for signals made by others, remember that cyclists may signal right turns by holding their right arms straight out.

After signalling, move only when it is safe to do so.

Keep right

Keep to the right of the road or in the right-hand lane on multi-lane roads unless you want to turn left or pass another vehicle. This is especially important if you are driving more slowly than other vehicles.

Obey speed limits

Obey the maximum speed limit posted on signs along the road, but always drive at a speed that will let you stop safely. This means driving below the maximum speed in bad weather, in heavy traffic or in construction zones. School zones and construction zones often have lower speed limits to protect children and those who work on or near the road.

Where there are no posted speed limits, the maximum speed is 50 km/h in cities, towns, and villages and 80 km/h elsewhere.

Cruise control is a driver aid that can improve fuel economy and prevent you from inadvertently exceeding the speed limit. However, there are some circumstances in which cruise control should not be used, such as adverse driving conditions (wet, icy or slippery roads), in heavy traffic, or when you are feeling fatigued.

Speed measuring warning devices are illegal. If you get caught driving with such a device, you will be fined and accumulate demerit points.

Obey police

When police officers are directing traffic, you must follow their directions, even if the directions are different from traffic lights or signs.

When a police officer signals you to pull your vehicle over, you must pull over as far to the right as you safely can and come to a complete stop. Stay in your vehicle and wait for the police officer. You must immediately, upon the police officer's request, surrender your driver's licence, vehicle permit (or copy) and insurance. Contrary to popular belief, you do not have 24 hours to present these documents. If you do not obey a police officer's direction to pull over, you risk being fined (up to $25,000), having your licence suspended or even serving time in prison.

To give yourself a two-second space, follow these steps:

1. Pick a marker on the road ahead, such as a road sign or telephone pole
2. When the rear of the vehicle ahead passes the marker, count "one thousand and one, one thousand and two".
3. When the front of your vehicle reaches the marker, stop counting. If you reach the marker before you count "one thousand and two," you are following too closely.

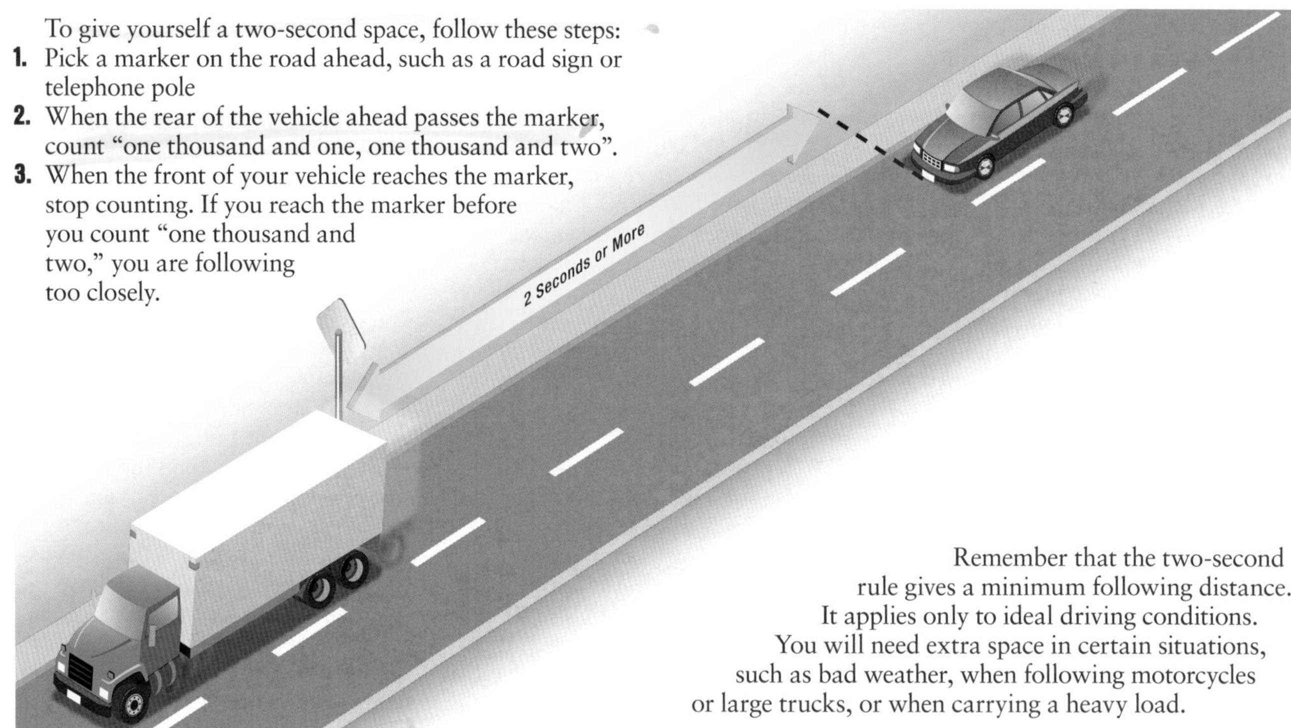

Remember that the two-second rule gives a minimum following distance. It applies only to ideal driving conditions. You will need extra space in certain situations, such as bad weather, when following motorcycles or large trucks, or when carrying a heavy load.

Diagram 2-9

Maintaining space

As a general rule, drive at the same speed as traffic around you without going over the speed limit. Leave a cushion of space around your vehicle to let other drivers see you and to avoid a collision.

Whenever you follow another vehicle, you need enough space to stop safely if the other vehicle brakes suddenly. A safe following distance is at least two seconds behind the vehicle in front of you. This lets you see around the vehicle ahead and gives you enough distance to stop suddenly.

Do not block the normal and reasonable movement of traffic.

Chapter 2, section II — Summary

By the end of this section you should know:

- How to steer and use your vehicle's signalling system and hand signals
- The importance of maintaining space and how to measure following distance
- Where to position your vehicle on the road and to obey speed limits and police

III. Sharing the road with other road users

Ontario's roads accommodate a variety of road users, including pedestrians, motorcycles, limited-speed motorcycles, mopeds, bicycles, large trucks, buses and farm machinery. Be aware of other road users, the speed at which they travel and the space they occupy on the road.

Sharing the road with motorcycles and limited-speed motorcycles

Motorcycles, limited-speed motorcycles, mopeds and bicycles are harder to see because of their size. Drivers of these vehicles may make sudden moves because of uneven road surfaces or poor weather conditions. Because they are less protected, they are more likely to be injured in a collision.

Motorcycles use a full lane; treat them like other vehicles when driving. Since many motorcycle turn signals do not automatically shut off, be careful when turning left in front of an oncoming motorcycle with its turn signal on. Make sure the motorcyclist is actually turning; he or she may have just forgotten to switch off the turn signal.

Sharing the road with cyclists

Bicycles and mopeds that cannot keep up with other traffic are expected to ride one meter from the curb or parked cars, or as close as practicable to the right hand edge of the road when there is no curb. However, they can use any part of the lane if necessary for safety, such as to:

- avoid obstacles, debris, potholes and sewer grates;
- cross railway or streetcar tracks at a 90° angle; and
- discourage passing where the lane is too narrow to be shared safely.

Cyclists are not required to ride close to the right edge of the road when they are travelling at or faster than the normal speed of traffic at that time and place, or when they are getting in position to turn left or turning left. (Cyclists are permitted to make a left turn from a left turn lane, where one is available.)

When passing a cyclist, allow at least one metre between your car and the cyclist. Whenever possible, you should change lanes to pass.

When turning right, signal and check your mirrors and the blind spot to your right to make sure you do not cut off a cyclist. When parked on the side of the street, look behind you and check your mirrors and blind spots for a passing cyclist before opening a door.

Sharing the road with large commercial vehicles

It is extremely important to know how to drive safely when sharing the road with large commercial vehicles such as tractor-trailers and buses. Recent data shows that the majority of fatalities resulting from collisions involving large commercial trucks are not the result of the truck driver's actions but of the other driver's actions. Therefore, sharing the road

Diagram 2-10

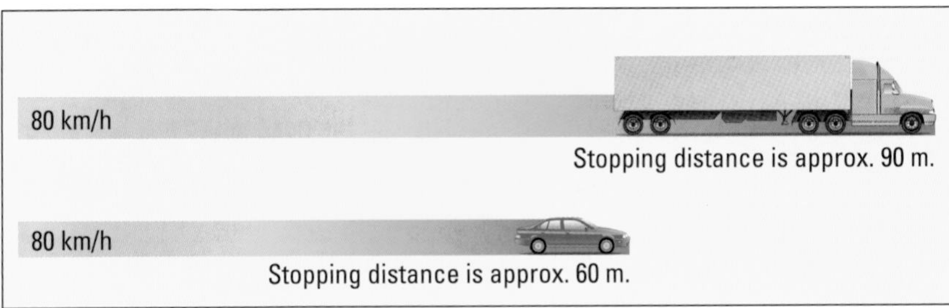
80 km/h
Stopping distance is approx. 90 m.
80 km/h
Stopping distance is approx. 60 m.

Diagram 2-11

with large commercial vehicles means you must always be aware of a large vehicle's capabilities and limitations. Be aware of the following:

1. **Blind Spots** — Large commercial vehicles have big blind spots on both sides. Avoid tailgating a large vehicle. The driver cannot see you if you are directly behind and if the vehicle stops suddenly, you have no place to go. Remember that if you can't see the driver's face in the large vehicle's side view mirror, the driver cannot see you.
2. **Stopping Distance** — Large commercial vehicles require a much longer distance to stop than smaller vehicles. When passing a large vehicle, do not cut in front closely. Not only is this discourteous, it is dangerous; it reduces the space cushion large vehicles require in order to stop safely. Allow more room when passing a large vehicle.
3. **Wide Turns** — When making a right turn, a large vehicle may need to first swing wide to the left and around in order to avoid hitting the right curb. If a large vehicle in front of you is making a right turn, do not move up into the space that opens up in the right lane; you are putting yourself into a very dangerous position. Once the front of the vehicle has cleared the corner, the rest will move partially back into the right lane. If you are in that lane, your vehicle will be squeezed between the trailer and the curb. Stay well back until the truck has completely cleared the lane.

   This situation can occur on expressway off-ramps that have two left turning lanes. Do not drive up into the left lane when a large vehicle is making a left turn in front of you. Stay well back until the truck has cleared the left turn, or else you may get squeezed between the truck and the curb.
4. **Rolling Back** — Leave plenty of

room if you are stopped behind a large vehicle. When the driver of a large vehicle releases the brakes after being stopped, the vehicle may roll back.

5. **Spray** — In bad weather, large vehicles are capable of spraying up large amounts of mud, snow and debris, which could land on your windshield and temporarily block your vision.
6. **Turbulence** — Due to various factors such as air pressure and airflow, a large vehicle can create heavy air turbulence. This may affect your ability to control your vehicle when passing a large vehicle.

Sharing the road with municipal buses

Many municipal roadways have special indented stopping areas for municipal buses, called bus bays, where passengers can get on and off. There are three types of bus bays:

- mid-block indented bays;
- indentations immediately before and after intersections; and
- bus stop areas between two designated parking areas.

When a bus in a bus bay begins flashing its left turn signals, indicating that it is ready to leave the bus bay, and you are approaching in the

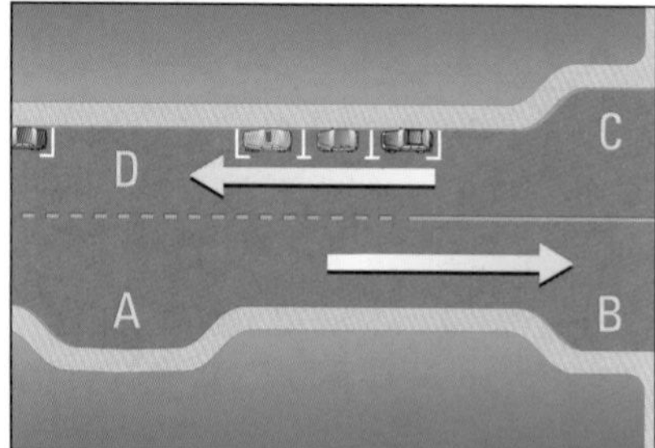

Diagram 2-12

A Mid - block indented bays
B An indentation before an intersection
C An indentation after an intersection
D Bus stops between legally parked cars

lane adjacent to the bus bay, you must allow the bus to re-enter traffic.

Sharing the road with farm machinery

Farm machinery moves quite slowly compared to other road users. Most tractors and combines have a maximum speed of 40 km/h, but travel at less than 40 km/h when towing implements or wagons. Farm machinery is often oversized, wide or long or both, making it difficult for the driver to see vehicles coming up from behind. Farmers often turn directly into fields rather than roads or lanes, or move from lane to lane. Remember that it is common for farmers to be on the roads after dark during peak planting and harvesting seasons.

Farm machinery on the road must display an orange and red slow-moving vehicle sign on the rear of the vehicle. The sign warns other drivers that the vehicle is travelling at 40 km/h or less. If you see one of these signs, slow down and be cautious. Stay well back and do not pass until it is safe to do so. (See the slow-moving vehicle sign on page 109.)

Sharing the road with pedestrians

Pay special attention to pedestrians, whether they are crossing roads in traffic, walking or jogging alongside roads, or using crosswalks or crossovers (generally known as crossings). Watch for children. Drive slowly and cautiously through school zones, residential areas and any other area where children may be walking or playing. You never know when a child might dart out from between parked cars or try to cross a street without checking for oncoming traffic. Be very cautious at twilight when children may still be playing outside, but are very difficult to see. Watch out for Community Safety Zone signs as they indicate areas where the community has identified that there is a special risk to pedestrians.

Seniors or pedestrians with disabilities need extra caution and courtesy from drivers as they may be slow in crossing the road. Be alert for pedestrians who are blind, with a visual or hearing disability, people who use wheelchairs or people walking slowly due to some other physical disabilities and give them appropriate consideration. Pedestrians who are blind or with a visual disability may use a white cane or guide dog to help them travel safely along sidewalks and across intersections. Caution signs are posted in some areas where there is a special need for drivers to be alert.

Persons operating mobility devices (motorized wheelchair and medical scooters) are treated the same way as pedestrians. Usually these operators will travel along a sidewalk but if there is no sidewalk available, persons using a mobility device should travel, like pedestrians, along the left shoulder of the roadway facing oncoming traffic.

Some streetcar stops have a special safety island or zone for passengers getting on and off. Pass these safety islands and zones at a reasonable speed. Always be ready in case pedestrians make sudden or unexpected moves.

Chapter 2, section III — Summary

By the end of this section you should know:

- The importance of sharing the road with other road users, especially large vehicles, cyclists, and pedestrians
- How to share the road with other road users safely and appropriately

IV. Driving through intersections

Be alert as you come to intersections and look carefully for pedestrians, cyclists, other motor vehicles, yield signs, stop signs and traffic lights. Be sure to scan any sidewalks and paths/trails as well as the roadways. Bear in mind that children are often unaware of traffic laws and also that cycling on the sidewalk may be permitted by local by-law.

There are two main types of intersections: controlled and uncontrolled.

Controlled intersections

Controlled intersections have traffic lights, yield signs or stop signs to control traffic (Diagram 2-14).

At a controlled intersection where you face a green light, drive carefully through the intersection at a steady speed. If the light has been green for a while, be prepared to stop when it turns yellow. However, if you are already so close that you cannot stop safely, drive through the intersection with caution. Where you face a red light, come to a complete stop and wait until the light turns green.

When you approach an intersection on a main road, and the intersection is blocked with traffic, stop before entering the intersection and wait until the traffic ahead moves on. This does not apply if you are turning left or right.

At a controlled intersection where you face a yield sign, slow down or stop if necessary and wait until the way is clear before driving through the intersection.

At a controlled intersection where you face a stop sign, come to a complete stop. Drive through the intersection only when the way is clear (Diagram 2-14).

Uncontrolled intersections

Uncontrolled intersections have no signs or traffic lights. They are usually found in areas where there

Diagram 2-13

Diagram 2-14

is not much traffic. Be extra careful around these intersections. If two vehicles come to an uncontrolled intersection from different roads at the same time, the driver on the left must let the driver on the right go first. This is called yielding the right-of-way.

Yielding the right-of-way

There are times when you must yield the right-of-way. This means you must let another driver go first. Here are some rules about when you must yield the right-of-way.

At an intersection without signs or lights, you must yield the right-of-way to a vehicle approaching the intersection before you, and if you arrive at the same time, the vehicle approaching from the right has the right-of-way (Diagram 2-13).

At an intersection with stop signs at all corners, you must yield the right-of-way to the first vehicle to come to a complete stop. If two vehicles stop at the same time, the vehicle on the left must yield to the vehicle on the right (Diagram 2-14).

Diagram 2-15

At any intersection where you want to turn left or right, you must yield the right-of-way. If you are turning left, you must wait for approaching traffic to pass or turn and for pedestrians in or approaching your path to cross. If you are turning right, you must wait for pedestrians to cross if they are in or approaching your path (Diagram 2-15). You should also check your blind spot for cyclists approaching from behind, particularly in a bike lane to your right, on sidewalk or trail. A yield sign means you must slow down or stop if necessary and yield the right-of-way to traffic in the intersection or on the intersecting road.

Diagram 2-16

When entering a road from a private road or driveway, you must yield to vehicles on the road and pedestrians on the sidewalk (Diagram 2-16).

Diagram 2-17

You must yield the right-of-way to pedestrians crossing at specially marked pedestrian crossovers (Diagram 2-17).

Remember, signalling does not give you the right-of-way. You must make sure the way is clear.

Chapter 2, section IV — Summary

By the end of this section you should know:

- The difference between controlled and uncontrolled intersections and how to safely navigate them
- The concept of right-of-way and common situations where you must yield to other road users

V. Stopping

Diagram 2-18

Diagram 2-19

Knowing how to stop safely and properly is an important driving skill. Safe and responsible drivers see stops ahead, check their mirrors, begin braking early and stop smoothly. Braking is easier when you sit properly. Use your right foot for both brake and gas pedals so you won't step on both pedals at the same time or activate your brake lights unnecessarily. Press the brake pedal firmly and evenly.

In a vehicle with manual transmission, try shifting into a lower gear going down long, steep hills. This will help control your speed and you won't have to brake as sharply. Downshift before starting downhill since it may not be possible once you are going downhill. As a guide, you should be in the same gear going downhill as uphill.

You must come to a complete stop for all stop signs and red traffic lights. Stop at the stop line if it is marked on the pavement (Diagram 2-18).

If there is no stop line, stop at the crosswalk, marked or not. If there is no crosswalk, stop at the edge of the sidewalk. If there is no sidewalk, stop at the edge of the intersection (Diagram 2-19). Wait until the way is clear before entering the intersection.

Stopping at railway crossings

All railway crossings on public roads in Ontario are marked with large red and white 'X' signs. Watch for these signs and be prepared to stop. You may also see yellow advance warning signs and large 'X' pavement markings ahead of railway crossings. Some railway crossings have flashing signal lights and some use gates or barriers to keep drivers from crossing the tracks when a train is coming. Some less travelled crossings have stop signs posted. Remember it can take up to two kilometres for a train to stop under full emergency braking. On private roads, railway crossings may not be marked, so watch carefully.

Diagram 2-20

When you come to a railway crossing, remember:

- Slow down, listen and look both ways to make sure the way is clear before crossing the tracks.
- If a train is coming, stop at least five metres from the nearest rail or gate. Do not cross the track until you are sure the train or trains have passed.
- Never race a train to a crossing.
- If there are signal lights, wait until they stop flashing and, if the crossing has a gate or barrier, wait until it rises, before you cross the tracks.
- Never drive around, under or through a railway gate or barrier while it is down, being lowered or being raised. It is illegal and dangerous.
- Avoid stopping in the middle of railway tracks; for example, in heavy traffic, make sure you have enough room to cross the tracks completely before you begin to cross.
- Avoid shifting gears while crossing tracks.
- If you get trapped on a crossing, immediately get everyone out and away from the vehicle. Move to a safe place and then contact authorities.
- Buses and other public vehicles are required to stop at railway crossings that are not protected by gates, signal lights, or a stop sign. School buses must stop at railway crossings whether or not they are protected by gates or signal lights. Watch for these buses and be prepared to stop behind them.
- If you are approaching a railway crossing with a **stop sign**, you must stop unless otherwise directed by a flagman.

Stopping at school crossings

Where a school crossing guard displays a red and white stop sign you must stop before reaching the crossing and remain stopped until all persons, including the school crossing guard, have cleared your half of the roadway and it is safe to proceed. If you have any doubts on when it is safe to drive forward, wait until all the children and the guard have cleared the crossing. Drivers who don't follow the stopping requirements may be fined between $150 and $500 and get 3 demerit points.

Stopping for school buses

School buses in Ontario come in a range of sizes. All are chrome yellow and display the words "School Bus."

You must stop whenever you approach a stopped school bus with its upper alternating red lights flashing, regardless of whether you are behind the bus or approaching it from the front. When approaching the bus from the front, stop at a safe distance for children to get off the bus and cross the road in front of you. If you are coming from behind the bus, stop at least 20 metres away. Do not go until the bus moves or the lights have stopped flashing.

If you are on a road with a median strip, only vehicles coming from behind the bus must stop. (A median is a physical barrier such as a raised, lowered, earth or paved strip constructed to separate traffic travelling in different directions. Vehicles cannot cross over a median strip.)

You must obey the school bus law on any road, no matter how many lanes or what the speed limit. Be prepared to stop for a school bus at any time, not just within school hours.

As well as the upper alternating red flashing lights, school buses use a stop sign arm on the driver's side of the bus. This arm, a standard stop sign with alternating flashing red lights at top and bottom, swings out after the upper alternating red lights begin to flash. Remain stopped until the arm folds away and all lights stop flashing.

Diagram 2-21

Diagram 2-22

Note: It is illegal to fail to stop for a stopped school bus that has its red lights flashing. If you don't stop, you can be fined $400 to $2,000 and get six demerit points for a first offence. If you are convicted a second time within five years, the penalty is a fine of $1,000 to $4,000 and six demerit points. You could also go to jail for up to six months. In Ontario, school bus drivers and other witnesses can report vehicles that have illegally passed a school bus. If you are the vehicle's registered owner, these same fines, but not demerit points or jail time, may be applied to you.

Watch for school buses near railway crossings. All school buses must stop at all railway crossings. The upper alternating red lights are not used for these stops, so be alert.

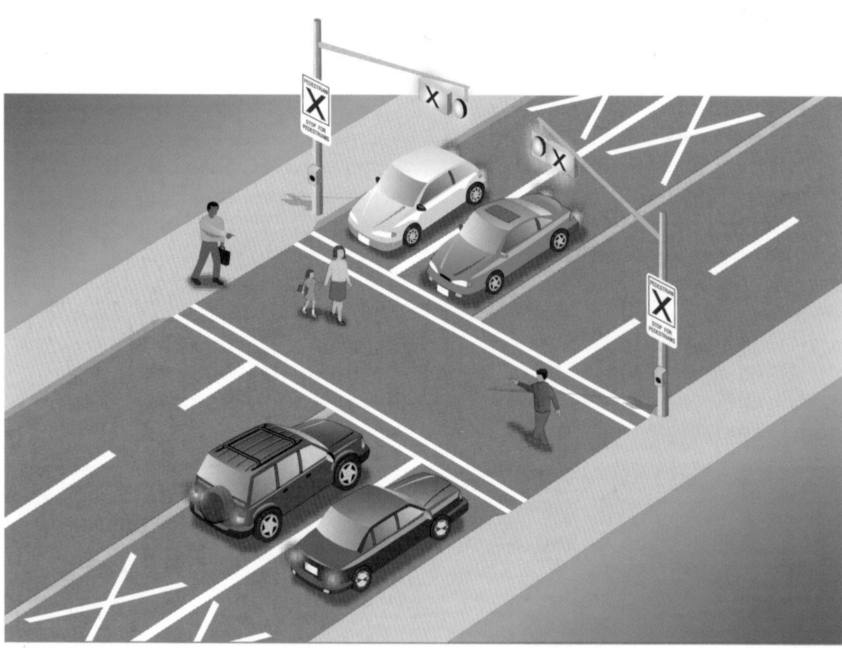

Diagram 2-23

Stopping for pedestrian crossovers

Pedestrian crossovers (also commonly called crosswalks) are designated areas that allow pedestrians to safely cross roads where there are no traffic lights. Always watch for pedestrians and people using wheelchairs at these crossings.

Pedestrians may push a button to make the overhead yellow lights flash to warn drivers that they will be crossing. Pedestrians should point or make an indication to drivers that they want to cross before entering the roadway (try making eye contact when possible). Drivers including cyclists must yield the right-of-way to pedestrians in the crossover. Once people have cleared your side of the road, and no other pedestrians are approaching, you may proceed with caution when it is safe. You must not pass any vehicle within 30 metres of a pedestrian crossover.

Chapter 2, section V — Summary

By the end of this section you should know:

- Where to position your vehicle when stopping at stop lights and stop signs
- The importance of stopping at railway crossings and how to position your vehicle to stop for them
- How and when to stop for school crossings and school buses
- How and when to stop for pedestrian crossovers

VI. Changing directions

Before you turn a corner, back up, change lanes or turn around, you need to know what is beside and behind you. Always check your mirrors and over your shoulder to make sure the way is clear and you have enough space to complete the move safely.

Turning a corner

To turn a corner, signal well before the turn. When the way is clear, move into the proper lane, either the far right lane for a right turn or the far left lane in your direction for a left turn. Signal your turn and look from side to side and check your blind spots to make sure the way is clear.

Slow down before you enter the turn; the sharper the turn, the slower you should go. To keep full control of the vehicle, finish braking before you turn the steering wheel.

For a sharp turn, turn the steering wheel with one hand and cross

Diagram 2-24

the other hand over it. Grip the wheel on the other side and continue turning. This is called "hand over hand steering." When you have completed the turn, relax your grip on the steering wheel and let it slip or gently feed it through your hands to return to the straight-ahead position. Do not turn the steering wheel with one finger or the flat palm of your hand. Gradually increase speed as you complete the turn.

Remember, drivers often lose control of vehicles and skid because they try to do more than one thing at a time. Try not to brake and steer at the same time (unless you vehicle is equipped with anti-lock brakes).

Right turns

Unless signs or pavement markings tell you not to, always begin and end a right turn close to the right side of the road.

To make a right turn, signal well before the turn and move into the right-hand lane when the way is clear. If the right-hand lane is not marked, keep as far to the right of the road as possible. Look ahead, left, right and left again before starting to turn. If you have not seen any smaller vehicles or pedestrians, check your right rear blind spot. Let cyclists, limited-speed motorcycles, or moped riders go through the intersection before you turn. When it is safe, complete your turn into the right-hand lane of the road you are entering.

Right turn on a red light

Unless a sign tells you not to, you may make a right turn facing a red light as long as you first come to a complete stop and wait until the way is clear. Remember to signal your turn and yield to pedestrians and others using the road.

Left turns

Unless signs or pavement markings tell you not to, always begin and end a left turn in the far left lane in your direction.

To make a left turn, signal well before the turn and move into the far left lane when the way is clear. Look ahead, behind, left, right and left again and check your blind spots. Make your turn when the way is clear.

When you are stopped at an intersection waiting for approaching traffic to clear, don't turn your steering wheel to the left until you can complete the turn. With your wheels turned to the left, your vehicle could be pushed into the

The following diagrams show you the correct way to turn left on different types of roads:

Diagram 2-25: Two-way road to a two-way road
Turn from the left lane closest to the centre line to the lane right of the centre line, following a smooth arc. Then, when you can, move into the right curb lane.

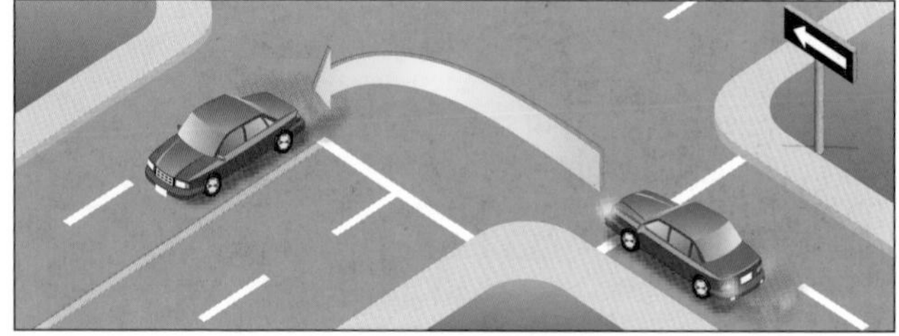

Diagram 2-27: One-way road to a two-way road
Turn from the left curb lane to the lane just right of the centre line. Then, when you can, move into the right curb lane.

Diagram 2-26: Two-way road to a one-way road
Turn from the lane closest to the centre line to the left curb lane.

Diagram 2-28: One-way road to a one-way road
Turn from the left curb lane to the left curb lane.

path of oncoming traffic.

When two vehicles coming from opposite directions meet in an intersection waiting to turn left, each should turn to the left of the other after yielding the right-of-way to pedestrians and oncoming traffic.

Motorcycles, bicycles, limited-speed motorcycles and mopeds turn left at intersections in the same way as larger vehicles. If you are making a left turn behind one of these vehicles, do not pull up beside it to make your turn at the same time. Stay behind and turn when the way is clear. Wait for the smaller vehicle to move right before you pass.

Left-turn lanes

Some roads have special lanes for vehicles turning left (Diagram 2-29). At an intersection where left-turn lanes are marked on the pavement, make your turn from the marked lane. Keep this lane position as you turn onto the other road.

Diagram 2-29

The centre lane of some roads is used as a two-way left-turn lane (Diagram 2-30). This lets left-turning vehicles from both directions wait for a chance to turn without holding up traffic. To use a two-way left-turn lane, follow these steps:

1. Signal and move into the centre lane shortly before your turn. Slow down.
2. Carefully move forward to a spot opposite the road or driveway where you want to turn.
3. Make your turn when the way is clear.

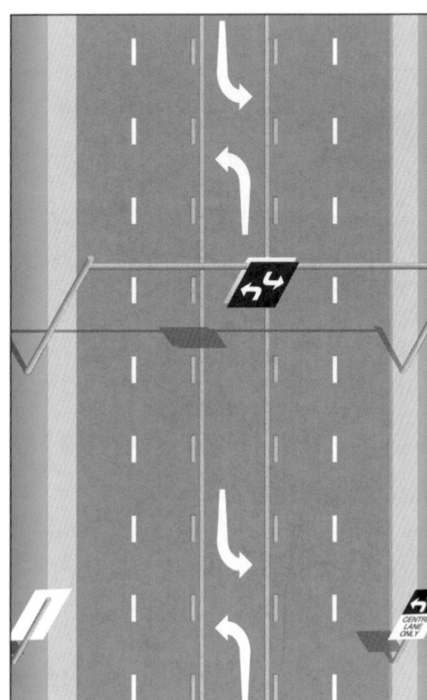

Diagram 2-30

Remember that vehicles from the opposite direction also use this lane to turn left. As they wait in front of you, it may be hard for you to see oncoming traffic. Only go when you are sure the way is clear. These left turn lanes are not to be used for passing.

Left turn on a red light

You may turn left from a one-way road to a one-way road on a red light after coming to a complete stop and making sure the way is clear. Yield to pedestrians and traffic.

Driving through roundabouts

Approaching:

- **Slow down** and watch for pedestrians on the approach to the yield line at the entrance of the roundabout. Stay in your lane.

Entering:

- **Visual checks:** Do visual checks of all vehicles already in the roundabout and those waiting to enter (including cyclists).
- **Look left:** Traffic in the roundabout has the right-of-way. When preparing to enter the roundabout, pay special attention to the vehicles to your left. Adjust your speed or stop at the yield sign if necessary.
- **Adequate gap:** Watch for a safe opportunity to enter the roundabout. Enter when there is an adequate gap in the circulating traffic flow. Don't enter directly beside another vehicle already in the roundabout, as that vehicle may be exiting at the next exit.
- **Travel counter-clockwise:** Once in the roundabout, always keep to the right of the central island and travel in a counter-clockwise direction.
- **Keep moving:** Once you are in the roundabout, do not stop except to avoid a collision; you have the right-of-way over entering traffic.
- **Signal:** Always signal lane changes.

Exiting:

- **Signal:** Be sure to signal your exit and watch for pedestrians.
- **Maintain your lane:** Stay to the left if you entered from the left lane, or stay to the right if you entered from the right lane.
- **Maintain your position:** Maintain your position relative to other vehicles.
- **Signal intent to exit:** Once you have passed the exit before the one you want, use your right-turn signal.
- **Left lane exit:** If exiting from the left lane, watch out for vehicles on the right that continue to circulate around the roundabout.

Dealing with particular situations at a roundabout:

Consider large vehicles

Allow extra room alongside large vehicles (trucks and buses). Large vehicles may have to swing wide on the approach or within the roundabout. Give them plenty of room.

Diagram 2-31: Two-laned Roundabout.

Pull over for emergency vehicles

If you are in a roundabout when an emergency vehicle approaches, exit at your intended exit and proceed beyond the traffic island before pulling over. If you have not entered the roundabout yet, pull over to the right if possible and wait until the emergency vehicle has passed.

Driving a large vehicle in a roundabout

A driver negotiating a roundabout in a large vehicle (such as a truck or bus) may need to use the full width of the roadway, including the apron (a mountable portion of the centre island adjacent to the roadway) if provided. Prior to entering the roundabout, the vehicle may need to occupy both lanes. Give large vehicles plenty of room to manoeuvre.

Backing up

Take extra care and move slowly when backing up (reversing) your vehicle. Before you begin, check that the way is clear behind you. Be especially careful to look for children and cyclists.

While firmly holding the steering wheel, put the gear selector in reverse and turn sideways in your seat to look over your shoulder in the direction you are moving. If you are reversing straight back or to the right, turn your body and head to the right and look back over your right shoulder (Diagram 2-32). If you are reversing to the left, turn your body and head to the left and look over your left shoulder (Diagram 2-33). Always check the opposite shoulder as well. If you are turning as you reverse, check that the front end of your vehicle does not hit anything.

You don't have to wear a seatbelt while backing up. If you need to remove your seatbelt to turn your body to see properly when reversing, do so. But don't forget to buckle up again before moving forward.

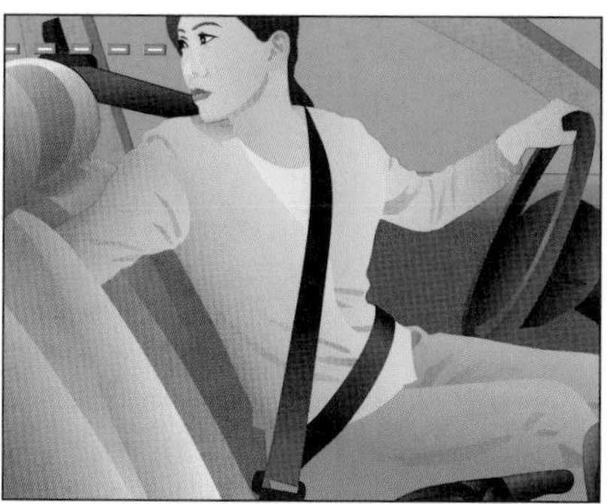

Diagram 2-32

It is illegal to drive in reverse on a divided road that has a speed limit of more than 80 km/h. This applies to the travelled section of the road and the shoulder. The only exception to this rule is if you are trying to help someone in trouble.

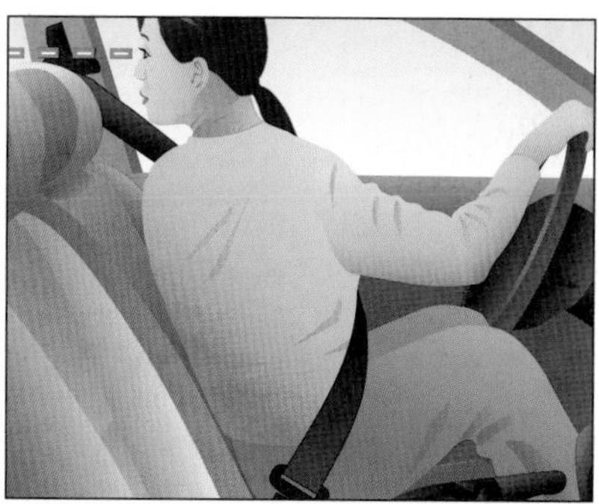

Diagram 2-33

Turning around

You may need to turn around when driving if you miss a turn or go too far along a road. There are several ways to do this safely.

The simplest and safest way is to drive around the block, but there may be times when this is not possible. In such cases, a U-turn or a three-point turn may be necessary.

U-turn

Before you make a U-turn, check to make sure there is no sign saying not to.

To make a U-turn safely, you must be able to see well in both directions. It is illegal to make a U-turn on a curve in the road, on or near a railway crossing or hilltop, or near a bridge or tunnel that blocks your view. Never make a U-turn unless you can see at least 150 metres in both directions.

To make a U-turn, signal for a right turn, check your mirror and over your shoulder and pull over to the right side of the road. Stop. Signal a left turn and when traffic is clear in both directions, move forward and turn quickly and sharply into the opposite lane. Check for traffic as you turn.

Three-point turn

On narrow roads you need to make a three-point turn to change directions. As shown in Diagram 2-34, a three-point turn starts from the far right side of the road. Make sure you do not make a three-point turn on a curve in the road, on or near a railway crossing or hilltop, or near a bridge or tunnel that blocks your view.

Signal for a left turn. When the way is clear in both directions, move forward, turning the steering wheel sharply left towards the curb on the far side of the road. When you have reached the left side of the road, stop. Shift the vehicle into reverse. Signal a right turn. After checking that the way is still clear, turn the steering wheel sharply to the right, while backing up slowly to the other side of the road. Stop. Shift to forward gear and check traffic. When the way is clear, drive forward.

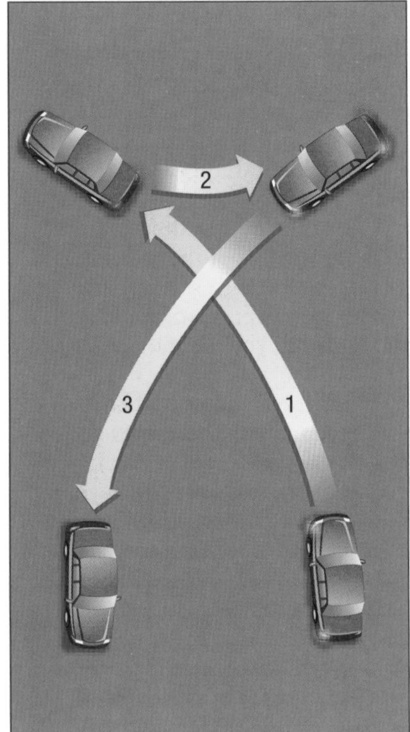

Diagram 2-34

Chapter 2, Section VI — Summary
By the end of this section you should know:
- How to properly turn left or right at intersections
- The rules surrounding turns onto and from one way streets
- How to navigate a roundabout
- Where to look and how to manoeuvre your vehicle when backing up
- Methods of turning your vehicle around to travel back in the opposite direction (U-turns, 3-point turns)

VII. Changing positions

Changing your position on the road involves changing lanes or overtaking and passing another vehicle. Before beginning, be sure you have enough space and time to complete the move safely.

Changing lanes

Changing lanes is a movement from one lane to another on roads with two or more lanes in the same direction. You may have to change lanes to overtake another vehicle, to avoid a parked vehicle or when the vehicle ahead slows to turn at an intersection.

Never change lanes without giving the proper signal and looking to make sure the move can be made safely.

Here are the steps for making a lane change:

1. Check your mirrors for a space in traffic where you can enter safely.
2. Check your blind spot by looking over your shoulder in the direction of the lane change. Be especially

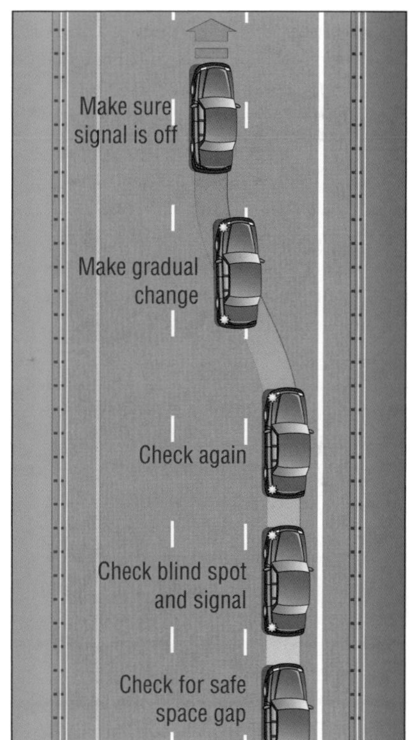
Make sure signal is off
Make gradual change
Check again
Check blind spot and signal
Check for safe space gap
Diagram 2-35

careful to check for bicycles and other small vehicles. Signal that you want to move left or right.
3. Check again to make sure the way is clear and that no one is coming too fast from behind or from two lanes over on a multi-lane road.
4. Steer gradually into the new lane. Do not slow down, maintain the same speed or gently increase it.

Never make sudden lane changes by cutting in front of another vehicle, including bicycles. Other drivers expect you to stay in the lane you are already in. Even if you signal, they expect you to yield the right-of-way.

Avoid unnecessary lane changes or weaving from lane to lane. You are more likely to cause a collision, especially in heavy traffic or bad weather. Don't change lanes in or near an intersection. Remember that spending a few seconds behind another vehicle is often safer than going around it.

Passing

Passing is changing lanes to move past a slower vehicle. While all public roads have speed limits, not all vehicles travel at the same speed. For example, cyclists, road service vehicles and drivers ahead that are preparing to turn are usually slower than the through traffic. You may want to pass some slow-moving vehicles when you are following them.

Never overtake and pass another vehicle unless you are sure you can do so without danger to yourself or others. Don't pass moving snow plows under any conditions. If in doubt, do not pass.

Here are the steps for passing a vehicle:

1. Use your left-turn signal to show that you want to pass and check that the way is clear ahead and behind before moving into the passing lane.
2. Watch for bicycles and small vehicles that may be hidden from

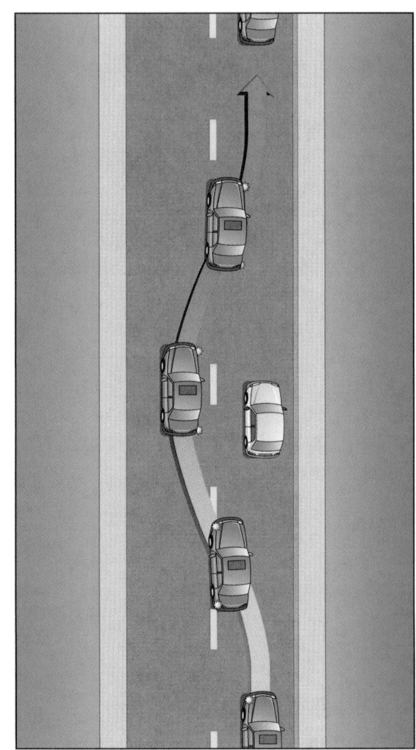

Diagram 2-36

view in front of the vehicle you are about to pass. Also watch for vehicles that may be turning left in front of you and vehicles or pedestrians entering the road from another road or driveway.
3. Change lanes only after signalling. After overtaking, signal that you want to move back into the lane you started from, and when you can see the entire front of the vehicle you are passing in your inside mirror, make the lane change. Be careful not to cut off a vehicle by suddenly moving in front of it.
4 If the vehicle you are passing speeds up, do not race. Go back to your original lane. And do not speed up when another driver is trying to pass you. It is unlawful and dangerous.

Passing within 30 metres of a pedestrian crossover is not permitted. Passing left of a centreline is not permitted 30 metres from a bridge, viaduct or tunnel. Don't attempt to pass when approaching the crest of a hill or on a curve where your vision of oncoming traffic is obstructed and there is not enough clear distance ahead to pass in safety.

When passing parked vehicles, watch carefully for people suddenly opening doors or for doors opened to load and unload.

Motorcycles, bicycles, limited-speed motorcycles and mopeds often need to pull to the left or right side of their lane to avoid dangerous road conditions or to be seen by other drivers. Do not take this as an invitation to pass in the same lane. If you do want to pass these vehicles, do so by changing lanes.

When faster traffic wants to pass you, move to the right and let it pass in safety. When being passed on an undivided road where the passing driver has pulled into the opposite

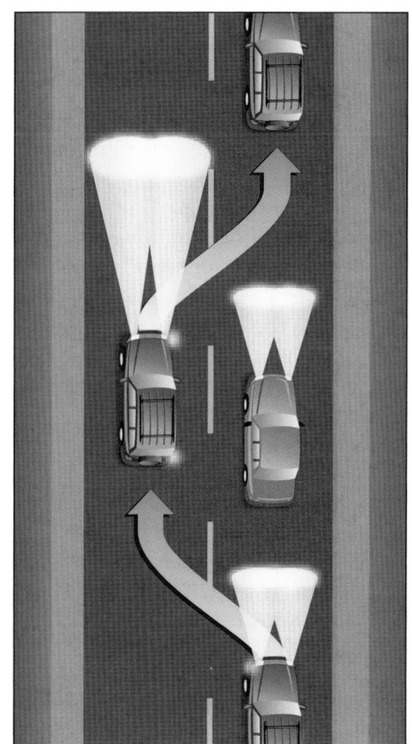

Diagram 2-37

lane, pay attention to oncoming traffic and move closer to the right side of the lane. Be prepared to slow down to let the passing driver get in front of you more quickly to prevent a collision.

On many high-speed roads with three or more lanes in each direction, trucks are not allowed to drive in the far left-hand lane. This means that the lane next to it is the truck passing lane. If you are in this lane and a truck wants to pass, move into the right-hand lane as soon as you can.

Passing at night

Be very careful when you pass other vehicles at night. If you have to pass and the way is clear, follow these steps:

1. Switch your headlights to low beams as you approach a vehicle from behind.
2. Signal, check your mirrors and blind spot, and pull out to pass. As you move alongside the vehicle you are passing, switch on your highbeams. This will let you see more of the road ahead.
3. When you can see all of the front of the vehicle you are passing in your rear view mirror, you are far enough ahead to pull back into the right lane. Remember to signal.

Diagram 2-38

Passing and climbing lanes

Some roads have special passing or climbing lanes. These lanes let slower vehicles move into the right-hand lane so that faster ones can pass safely in the left lane.

An advance sign tells drivers they will soon have a chance to pass.

Another sign warns when the lane is ending so drivers in the right-hand lane can begin to merge safely with traffic in the left-hand lane.

Passing on the shoulder

You may drive on the right shoulder only to pass a vehicle turning left and only if the shoulder is paved. You may not pass on the left shoulder, paved or not.

Passing on the right

Most passing is done on the left. You may pass on the right on multi-lane or one-way roads and when overtaking a streetcar or a left-turning vehicle.

Passing on the right can be more dangerous than passing on the left. If you are driving in the left most lane with a slower vehicle in front of you, wait for the vehicle to move to the right. Do not suddenly change lanes and pass on the right; the driver in front may realize you want to pass and move to the right at the same time you do.

Passing streetcars

You must pass streetcars on the right unless you are driving on a one-way road.

At streetcar stops, stay at least two metres behind the rear doors where passengers are getting off

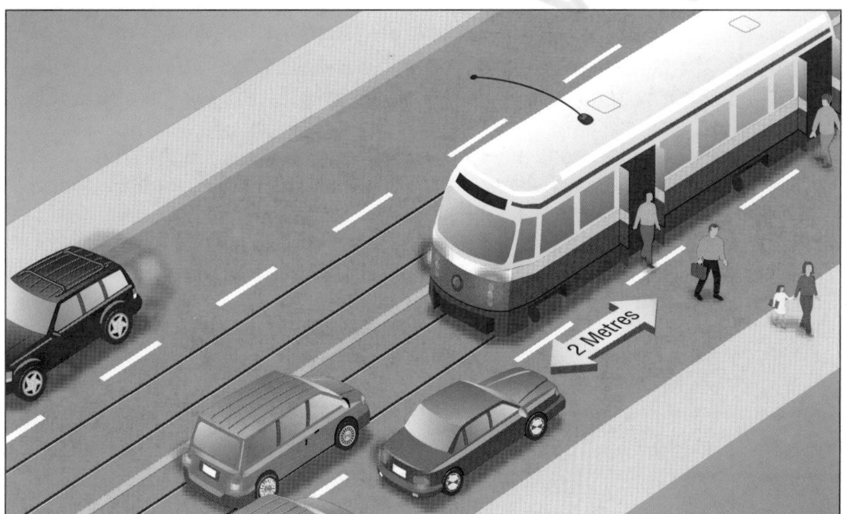

Diagram 2-39

or on. This rule does not apply at stops where an area has been set aside for streetcar passengers. Always pass these areas at a reasonable speed and be prepared for pedestrians to make sudden or unexpected moves.

Chapter 2, section VII — Summary

By the end of this section you should know:

- The safety considerations and the sequence of steps to follow when changing lanes or passing
- How to deal with specific situations when passing (e.g. at night, streetcars)

VIII. Parking along roadways

Since parking rules change from road to road and place to place, always watch for and obey signs that say you may not stop or limit stopping, standing or parking. Be aware that not all parking by-laws are posted on signs.

Here are some basic parking rules:

- Never park on the travelled part of a road. Drive off the road onto the shoulder if you must stop for some reason.
- Never park on a curve, hill or anywhere you do not have a clear view for at least 125 metres in both directions.
- Do not park where you will block a vehicle already parked or where you will block a sidewalk, crosswalk, pedestrian crossing or road entrance.
- Do not park within three metres of a fire hydrant, on or within 100 metres of a bridge or within six metres of a public entrance to a hotel, theatre or public hall when it is open to the public.
- Do not park within nine metres of an intersection or within 15 metres if it is controlled by traffic lights.
- Do not park within 15 metres of the nearest rail of a level railway crossing.
- Do not park where you will get in the way of traffic or snow clearing.
- Never open the door of your parked vehicle without first making sure that you will not endanger any other person or vehicle or interfere with traffic. Take extra precautions to avoid opening a door in the path of cyclists, who often ride close to parked cars (Diagram 2-40). When you must open a door next to traffic, keep it open only long enough to load or unload passengers.

After parking your vehicle, always turn off the ignition and the lights, remove the key and lock the door to deter theft. Do not leave children or

Diagram 2-40

animals in the vehicle.

Before moving from a parked position, always signal and check for traffic, pulling out only when it is safe to do so.

Parking for people with disabilities

The Accessible Parking Permit, formerly known as the Disabled Person Parking Permit, is a laminated card that may be displayed on the dashboard or turned-down sun visor of any vehicle in which a person with a disability is travelling. The permit entitles the vehicle in which the person named on the permit is travelling to park in designated disabled parking, standing and stopping areas. The permit is issued to the permit holder, not a specific vehicle.

People who have the old version of the permit, the Disabled Person Parking Permit, may continue to use this permit until it expires. Upon its expiry, any new permit issued will be the Accessible Parking Permit.

The Accessible Parking Permit is issued free of charge to qualified individuals. To qualify for an Accessible Parking Permit, a licensed physician, chiropractor, nurse practitioner (extended class), physiotherapist or occupational therapist must certify that the applicant has one or more of the conditions detailed on the Accessible Parking Permit application form.

There are four types of Accessible Parking Permits.

- A **regular permit** (blue) is issued to people with permanent disabilities and is valid for five years. Until 2011, all individuals will need to be recertified before renewing their permit. After that date, only individuals whose condition is deemed "subject to change" will need to be recertified before renewing their permit.

- A **temporary permit** (red) is issued when the disability is expected to last more than two months, but is not a permanent disability. The temporary permit is not renewable.
- A **traveller permit** (purple) is valid for up to one year and is issued upon request to individuals who hold a valid Accessible Parking Permit and plan to fly from any Ontario airport. The permit holder places the traveller permit on the dashboard or sun visor of their vehicle when leaving it parked at the airport. The person's regular permit travels with them.
- A **company permit** (green) is valid for up to five years and is issued to companies and non-profit organizations that own or lease vehicles used to transport people with physical disabilities.

Misuse or abuse of an Accessible Parking Permit should be reported to the police. Misuse of an Accessible Parking Permit will result in fines and revoked privileges.

Accessible Parking Permit applications are available on the Service Ontario Website http://www.ontario.ca/en/services_for_residents/ONT05_039815.html, at any Driver and Vehicle Licence Issuing Office or by sending a request to the ministry at the following address:

Service Ontario
Licence Renewals Unit
P.O. Box 9800
Kingston, ON K7L 5N8

Never park in a space designated for people with disabilities unless you display an Accessible Parking Permit in the windshield of your vehicle. The permit must belong to you or one of your passengers. This also applies to

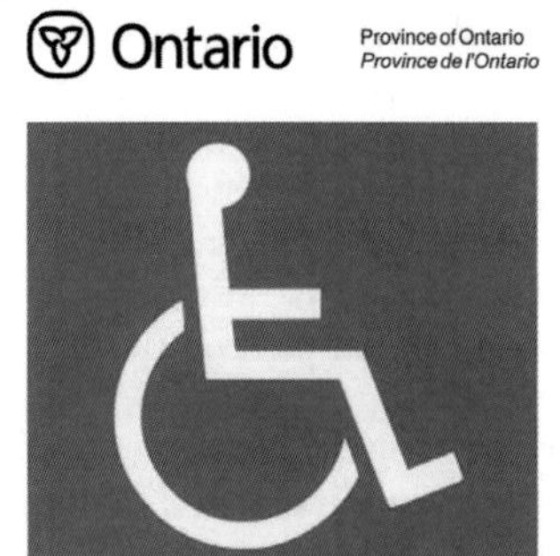

Diagram 2-41

standing or stopping at curb areas reserved for picking up and dropping off passengers with disabilities.

Parallel parking

Parallel parking means parking a vehicle with its wheels parallel and next to the curb or side of the road. Park parallel to the curb on roads where parking is allowed unless there are signs saying that vehicles should be parked at an angle. Park on the right side of the road in the direction of traffic. Unless there are signs saying otherwise, you can parallel park on both sides of a one-way road.

To parallel park on the right-hand side of the road, find a space that is about one and one half times longer than your vehicle. Check the traffic beside and behind and signal your wish to pull over and stop. Drive alongside, or parallel to, the vehicle ahead of the empty space, leaving about a metre between the vehicles. Stop when your rear bumper is in line with the other vehicle. Follow these steps:

Diagram 2-42

1. Slowly and carefully reverse into the space, turning the steering wheel fully towards the curb.
2. When you can see the outside rear corner of the vehicle in front of your space, straighten your wheels as you continue to reverse.
3. Turn the steering wheel fully toward the road to bring your vehicle in line with the curb.
4. If your vehicle is not parallel to the curb, drive forward to straighten.
5. When you are properly parked, set the parking brake and move the gear selector into park, or shift into first or reverse gear if your vehicle has a manual transmission.

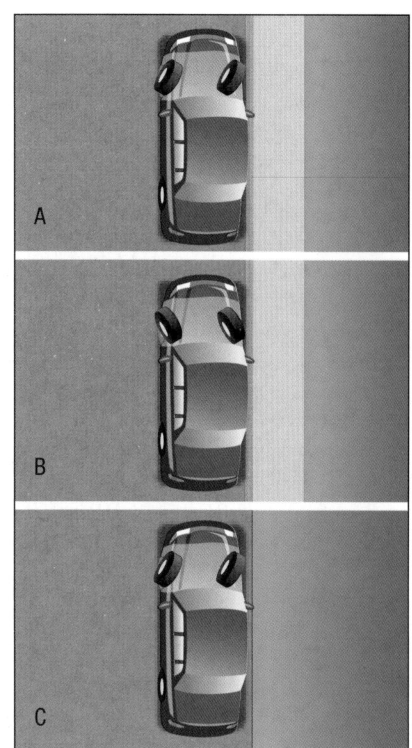

Diagram 2-43

6. Turn off the engine. Remember to remove the key from the ignition. Check traffic before opening your door. Lock your vehicle.

Parking on a hill

When parking facing downhill, turn your front wheels towards the curb or right shoulder. This will keep the vehicle from rolling into traffic if the brakes become disengaged (Diagram 2-43 A).

Turn the steering wheel to the left so the wheels are turned towards the road if you are facing uphill with a curb. The tires will catch the curb if it rolls backward (Diagram 2-43 B).

When facing uphill without a curb, turn the wheels sharply to the right. If the vehicle rolls, it will go off the road rather than into traffic (Diagram 2-43 C).

When parking on a hill, always set the parking brake and move the gear selector into park, or shift into first or reverse gear if your vehicle has a manual transmission. Turn off the engine and remove the key. Check for traffic before opening the door and remember to lock your vehicle.

Roadside stop

When you need to stop by the side of the road for a short time, to check something outside your vehicle or to look for directions on a map, for example, follow these directions:

1. Before slowing down, check your mirrors and blind spot to see when the way is clear.
2. Turn on your signal before slowing down unless there are vehicles waiting to enter the road from sideroads or driveways between you and the point where you intend to stop. Wait until you have passed these entrances so that drivers will not think you are turning before the stopping point.

3. Steer to the side of the road, steadily reducing speed, and stop parallel to the curb or edge of the road. You should not be more than about 30 centimetres away from it. Do not stop where you will block an entrance or other traffic.
4. Turn off your signal and turn on your hazard lights.

If your vehicle has an automatic transmission, put the gear selector in park and set the parking brake.
If your vehicle has a manual transmission, set the parking brake and shift into neutral if not turning off the engine, or shift into low or reverse if turning off the engine.
When parking on a hill, turn your wheels in the appropriate direction to keep your vehicle from rolling.

Pulling out from a roadside stop

When pulling out from a roadside stop, do the following:

1. Release the parking brake and move the gear selector to drive or shift into first gear.
2. Turn off your flashers and turn on your left turn signal.
3. Just before pulling away from the stop, check your mirrors and blind spot to make sure the way is clear of vehicles and cyclists.
4. Return to normal traffic speed by accelerating smoothly to blend with the traffic around you. In light traffic, accelerate moderately. In heavier traffic, you may have to accelerate more quickly. In a vehicle with manual transmission, shift gears as you increase speed.
5. Turn off your left turn signal as soon as you are back on the road.

Chapter 2, section VIII — Summary

By the end of this section you should know:

- Basic parking rules that may not appear on posted street signs
- What an Accessible Parking Permit is, and who is eligible to park in spaces designated for people with disabilities
- What parallel parking is and what steps to follow to complete it successfully
- How to safely pull over your vehicle for a roadside stop and re-enter traffic

IX. Freeway driving

A freeway — also called an expressway — is a high-speed, multi-lane road. On a freeway, traffic going in each direction is separated and ramps let vehicles enter and exit. Vehicle speed is higher on a freeway than on other roads, so driving can be more demanding and difficult. However, because there are no intersections, bicycles or pedestrians, freeway driving can be safer for experienced drivers.

New lanes called High Occupancy Vehicle (HOV) lanes are to be used for vehicles carrying a set minimum number of people. You will need to learn how to recognize markings and signs for these lanes, and the rules for using them.

New drivers need to learn how to drive with other vehicles around them at low speeds before trying freeway driving. Class G1 drivers may only drive on freeways with a licensed driving instructor.

Entering a freeway

There are usually two parts to a freeway entrance: an entrance ramp and an acceleration lane.

As you move along the freeway entrance ramp, look ahead and check your mirrors and blind spots to assess the traffic to see where you will move into the nearest freeway lane.

As you leave the ramp you enter the acceleration lane. In the acceleration lane, drivers increase their speed to the speed of traffic on the freeway before they merge with it. Signal and increase your speed to merge smoothly with traffic. Freeway drivers should move over, if it is safe to do so, leaving room for merging vehicles.

A few entrance ramps join the freeway on the left. This means you enter the fastest lane of traffic first. Use the acceleration lane to match your speed to the traffic, increasing your speed more quickly.

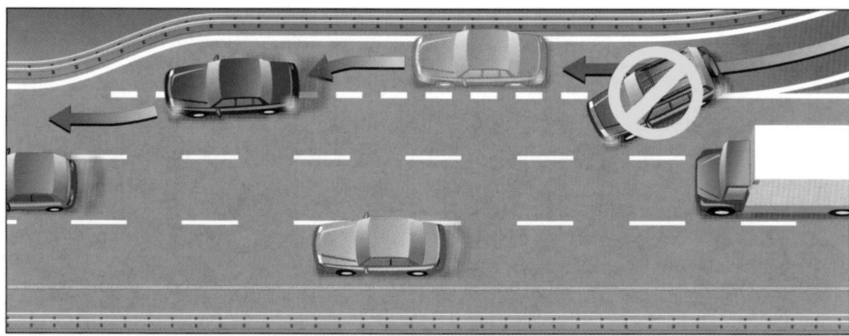

Diagram 2-44

Driving along a freeway

Once on the freeway, a safe driver travels at a steady speed, looking forward and anticipating what's going to happen on the road ahead. Traffic should keep to the right, using the left lanes for passing.

As in city driving, your eyes should be constantly moving, scanning the road ahead, to each side and behind. Look ahead to where you are going to be in the next 15 to 20 seconds, or as far ahead as you can see, when you travel at faster speeds. Remember to keep scanning and check your mirrors frequently.

Stay clear of large vehicles. Because of their size, they block your view more than other vehicles. Leave space around your vehicle. This will let you see clearly in every direction and will give you time and space to react. (See page 35 for correct following distances.)

Be careful not to cut off any vehicle, large or small, when making a lane change or joining the flow of traffic. It is dangerous and illegal for a slower moving vehicle to cut in front of a faster moving vehicle.

Use the far left lane of a multi-lane freeway to pass traffic moving slower than the speed limit, but don't stay there. Drive in the right-hand lane when possible. On many freeways with three or more lanes in each direction, large trucks cannot travel in the far left lane and must use the lane to the right for passing. Get into the habit of driving in the right lane, leaving the other lanes clear for passing.

Leaving a freeway

There are usually three parts to a freeway exit: a deceleration lane for slowing down that leads drivers out of the main flow of traffic, an exit ramp and an intersection with a stop sign, yield sign or traffic light.

Diagram 2-45

When leaving the freeway, signal that you want to move into the deceleration lane, but do not slow down. When you are in the lane, reduce your speed gradually to the speed shown for the exit ramp. Check your speedometer to make sure you are going slowly enough. You may not realize how fast you are going because you are used to the high speed of the freeway. Losing your ability to judge your speed accurately is sometimes called speed adaptation or velocitization. It is a special danger when leaving a freeway. Be prepared to stop at the end of the exit ramp.

Signs telling you that there are freeway exits ahead are far enough in advance for you to make any lane changes safely. If you miss an exit, do not stop or reverse on the freeway. Take the next exit.

High Occupancy Vehicle (HOV) lane

A High Occupancy Vehicle (HOV) lane is a specially designed lane that is designated for use by certain types of vehicles with a specified number of occupants. It can offer travel time savings to those who choose to carpool or take transit. HOV lanes can move a greater number of people than a general traffic lane, and encourage carpooling and transit use by providing travel time savings and a more reliable trip time. HOV lanes are open 24 hours a day, 7 days a week.

HOV lanes benefit all drivers, not only those who carpool, in the following ways:

- Improves highway infrastructure by moving more people in fewer cars;
- Reduces the number of vehicles on the road;
- Reduces overall vehicle emissions and improves air quality.

HOV lanes on provincial highways are reserved for vehicles carrying at least two people (i.e. a driver plus at least one passenger in any of the following passenger vehicles: cars, minivans, motorcycles, pickup trucks and buses).

- The HOV lane is separated from the other general traffic lanes by a striped buffer zone. It is illegal and unsafe to cross the striped buffer pavement markings.
- Certain vehicles are exempt from the HOV lane rules. Buses can use an HOV lane at any time, regardless of the number of occupants. Emergency vehicles such as police, fire and ambulance are also exempt from the restrictions.
- If you use the HOV lanes improperly, you can be stopped and ticketed by a police officer. You will be required to re-enter the general lanes at the next entry/exit zone.
- Commercial Motor Vehicles must have two or more persons in the vehicle and be less than 6.5 metres in total length to be in the HOV lane. Single-occupant taxis and airport limousines are permitted in

the HOV lane until June 30, 2015. Vehicles with the "Green" licence plate are permitted in the HOV lane with any number of occupants until June 30, 2015. Green plates are available for eligible plug-in hybrid electric vehicles and full battery electric vehicles. Please consult the Ministry of Transportation website for more details.

Chapter 2, section IX — Summary
By the end of this section you should know:
- What a freeway is and which road users can and cannot use them
- Safe practices to follow when entering, driving along or exiting a freeway
- What provincial freeway HOV lanes are and who can use them

X. Dealing with particular situations

Sanctions – dangerous behaviours

Our government is committed to protecting Ontarians from individuals who choose to engage in street racing, driving contests or driving stunts. Changes to the law went into effect on September 30, 2007. Drivers who are involved in street racing or aggressive driving behaviours can face tough sanctions:

- An immediate seven-day licence suspension and seven-day vehicle impoundment at roadside when a police officer has reasonable and probable grounds to believe the offence was committed;

If convicted:

- Fines from $2,000 to $10,000;
- Courts can impose a driver licence suspension of up to 10 years for a second conviction within 10 years;
- The accumulation of six demerit points, a maximum licence suspension of two years for a first conviction and a maximum 6 months in jail.

The use of a connected nitrous oxide system while driving on a highway is prohibited and the definition of a "stunt" includes speeding at 50 km/h or more above the posted limit.

The risk of a fatality or serious injury is almost five times greater for vehicles crashing at 50 km/h or more above the posted limit on a highway with a posted limit of 100 km/h. The increase in risk is even greater on roads with lower posted limits. For example, on roads with a posted limit of 60 km/h or less, the risk of a fatality or serious injury is almost eight times greater for vehicles colliding at 50 km/h or more above the posted limit.

Other dangerous behaviours are also now defined as stunts: driving in such a way that prevents another vehicle from passing, intentionally cutting off another vehicle, or intentionally driving too close to another vehicle, pedestrian or fixed object.

For information on the regulation, you can visit the following website www.search.elaws.gov.on.ca/en and search under current consolidated law for Highway Traffic Act - O. Reg. 339/94

Novice driver escalating sanctions

Escalating sanctions for novice drivers would apply if any of the following occurrences have taken place within a 5-year period:

- Any combination of repeat violations of G1/G2/M1/M2 restrictions;
- Convictions for individual HTA offences carrying four or more demerit points; or,
- Court ordered licence suspensions for HTA convictions that would have otherwise resulted in four or more demerit points.

Escalating sanctions for hybrid drivers would apply if there is any combination of repeat violations of their novice licence (G1/G2/M1/M2) conditions within a 5-year period.

The penalties under escalating sanctions for novice and hybrid drivers are:

- 30-day licence suspension for the first occurrence;
- 90-day licence suspension for the second occurrence; and
- Licence cancellation and a requirement to re-apply for a G1/M1 after the third occurrence. Any fees paid, credit received for time spent in the program or BDE credit would be forfeited when the licence is cancelled. Please note that in the case of a hybrid driver, only the novice class licence is cancelled on the third occasion, their full class licence is maintained.

A reinstatement fee is also imposed on first and second occurrence drivers.

Forfeited Fees:

If you prepaid any examination fees and are convicted for a third occurrence under escalating sanctions all your pre-paid fees will be lost. You will be required to pay all fees once you re-enter into the GLS program.

Note: If you are a novice driver and are convicted of violating any novice condition, an offence that is associated with 4 or more demerit points or receive a court-ordered suspension for an offence that would have resulted in 4 or more demerit points, you will receive the appropriate penalty and novice driver escalating sanction licence suspension. However, the demerit points will be recorded as zero on your record, and will not be counted towards the accumulated demerit point system.

Aggressive driving and road rage

Aggressive driving behaviours, such as tailgating, speeding, failing to yield the right of way and cutting in front of someone too closely, may cause other drivers to become frustrated and angry and lead to a road rage conflict between drivers. An angry driver may attempt dangerous retaliatory action. Avoid becoming angry on the road by following these tips:

- Know the warning signs of stress and combat them by getting fresh air, breathing deeply and slowly, and listening to relaxing music.
- Make a conscious decision not to take your problems with you when driving.
- If you are on a long trip, take a break from driving every few hours.
- Don't compete with another driver, or retaliate for what you believe to be inconsiderate behaviour.
- If someone else's driving annoys you, don't try to "educate" the person. Leave traffic enforcement to the police.
- Don't take other drivers' mistakes or behaviours personally.
- Avoid honking your horn at other drivers, unless absolutely necessary. A light tap on the horn is usually sufficient.

Remember that if you drive responsibly and courteously, you are less likely to spark a road rage situation.

- Plan your route in advance. Some of the most erratic and inconsiderate driving occurs when a driver is lost.
- Drive in a courteous and considerate manner.
- Yield the right-of-way when it is courteous to do so.
- Be polite and let other drivers in front of you when they are signalling that they would like to do so.
- If you make a mistake while driving, indicate that you are sorry. An apology can greatly reduce the risk of conflict.
- Don't return aggression. Avoid eye contact and do not gesture back. Keep away from erratic drivers.

If you are in a situation in which you feel threatened by another driver, do the following:

- Stay in your vehicle and lock the doors.
- If you have a cell phone, call police.
- Use your horn and signals to attract attention.
- If you believe you are being followed, do not drive home. Drive to a police station or a busy public place.

Street racing

Street racing is one of the most serious and reckless forms of aggressive driving. It shows a callous disregard for other drivers and road users, and it puts everyone on the road at serious risk of injury or death. Street racers run the risk of being charged under the *Criminal Code* of Canada.

Drowsy driving

Drowsiness has been identified as a causal factor in a growing number of collisions resulting in injury and fatality. Tired drivers can be as impaired as drunk drivers. They have a slower reaction time and are less alert.

Studies have shown that collisions involving drowsiness tend to occur during late night/early morning hours (between 2:00 a.m. and 6:00 a.m.) or late afternoon (between 2:00 p.m. and 4:00 p.m.). Studies also indicate that shift workers, people with undiagnosed or untreated sleep disorders, and commercial vehicle operators, are at greater risk for such collisions.

Always avoid driving when you are feeling drowsy. Scientific research confirms that you can fall asleep without actually being aware of it. Here are eight important warning signs that your drowsiness is serious enough to place you at risk:

- You have difficulty keeping your eyes open.
- Your head keeps tilting forward despite your efforts to keep your eyes on the road.
- our mind keeps wandering and you can't seem to concentrate.
- You yawn frequently.
- You can't remember details about the last few kilometres you have travelled.
- You are missing traffic lights and signals.
- Your vehicle drifts into the next lane and you have to jerk it back into your lane.
- You have drifted off the road and narrowly avoided a crash.

If you have one of these symptoms, you may be in danger of falling asleep. Pull off the road and park your vehicle in a safe, secure place. Use well-lit rest stops or truck stops on busy roads. Lock your doors, roll up your windows and take a nap.

Stimulants are never a substitute for sleep. Drinks containing caffeine can help you feel more alert, but if you are sleep deprived, the effects wear off quickly. The same is true of turning up the volume of your radio or CD player and opening the window. You cannot trick your body into staying awake; you need to sleep. Remember, the only safe driver is a well-rested, alert driver.

Workers on the road

Be extra careful when driving through construction zones and areas where people are working on or near the road.

When approaching a construction zone, proceed with caution and obey all warning signs, people and/or devices that are directing traffic through the area. Often, lower speed limits are posted to increase worker safety and reflect increased road hazards, such as construction vehicles in the area, uneven or gravel surfaces, narrowed lanes, etc. In the construction zone, drive carefully and adjust your driving to suit the conditions, do not change lanes, be ready for sudden stops and watch for workers and related construction vehicles and equipment on the road.

Other types of workers and vehicles may also be present on the road and pose a hazard, such as roadside assistance and disable vehicles, surveyors, road maintenance, or utility workers. Always, slow down and pass with caution to prevent a collision. If safe to do so, move over a lane to increase the space between your vehicle and the hazard.

Traffic control workers control vehicle traffic in work zones and prevent conflicts between construction activity and traffic. Whether you are driving during the day or at night, watch for traffic control people and follow their instructions.

Treat people working on roads with respect and be patient if traffic is delayed. Sometimes traffic in one direction must wait while vehicles from the other direction pass through a detour. If your lane is blocked and no one is directing traffic, yield to the driver coming from the opposite direction. When the way is clear, move slowly and carefully around the obstacle.

Recent changes to the Highway Traffic Act have resulted in doubled fines for speeding in a construction zone when workers are present. It is also an offence to disobey STOP or SLOW signs displayed by a traffic control person or firefighter.

Animals on the road

Crashes involving animals (mainly moose and deer) are a growing problem. Motor vehicle/wild animal collisions increased from 8,964 in 1999 to 12,791 collisions in 2008. This represents an increase of 43 per cent over a 10-year period. Many of these collisions go unreported.

You may encounter domestic, farm or wild animals on the road anywhere in Ontario. Scan the road ahead from shoulder to shoulder. If you see an animal on or near the road, slow down and pass carefully as they may suddenly bolt onto the road. Many areas of the province have animal crossing signs which warn drivers of the danger of large animals (such as moose, deer or cattle) crossing the road. Be cautious when you see these signs, especially during dusk to dawn hours when wild animals are most active.

To reduce your chances of hitting an animal:

- Reduce speed in darkness, rain and fog. These conditions can reduce your ability to see an animal on or near the road.
- Travel at a safe speed and stay alert. Driver inattention and speed are common factors in animal-vehicle crashes.
- Watch for shining eyes at the roadside. If you do see shining eyes, slow down and be ready to stop.
- Keep your windshield clean and headlights properly adjusted.

- Use high beams whenever possible and safe to do so and scan both sides of the road ahead.

If you see an animal:
- Slow down and sound your horn.
- Be alert for other animals which may be with the one you've seen.
- Don't try to drive around the animal. Animal movements are unpredictable.
- If you wish to watch an animal, find a safe place to pull completely off the road and park first. Do not park on the shoulder of the road, as other drivers may be distracted by the animal and hit your vehicle.
- Stay in your vehicle; getting out increases your chance of being hit by another vehicle.
- If you hit a deer or moose, report it to the local police service or the Ministry of Natural Resources. Do not try to move an injured animal.

Cellular phones

Cell phones can be an important safety aid for drivers, but using a cell phone while driving takes a driver's attention away from the task of driving and increases the risk of collision. Distracted drivers are more likely to make mistakes or react too slowly. That's why drivers who talk, text, type, dial or email using hand-held cell phones and other hand-held communications and entertainment devices face fines of up to $500 under Ontario's distracted driving law. Viewing display screens unrelated to driving, such as laptop computers and portable DVD players, is also prohibited while driving.

Police can also charge drivers with careless driving or even dangerous driving (a criminal offence) if they do not pay full attention to the driving task. If you are convicted of careless driving, you will get six demerit points and can be fined up to $2,000 and sentenced to up to six months in jail. In some cases, your licence may be suspended for up to two years.

Make it a habit to pull over and park to use your cell phone or have a passenger take the call or let it go to voice mail. If you must use a cell phone when driving, you must use it hands-free.

Driver distractions

Driving is a job that requires your full attention every time you get behind the wheel. Any secondary activity will detract from your ability to drive properly and safely. You must reduce distractions and focus on your driving.

There are a number of possible driver distractions including:
- Using devices such as GPS systems, stereos, CD and DVD players, radios, cell phones, laptops, PDA's and MP3 players;
- Reading maps, directions or other material;

Tips to reduce driver distractions

- Attend to personal grooming and plan your route before you leave.
- Identify and preset your vehicle's climate control, radio and CD player.
- Make it a habit to pull over and park to use your cell phone or have a passenger take the call or let it go to voice mail.
- Put reading material in the trunk if you are tempted to read.
- Do not engage in emotional or complex conversations.
- Stress can affect your driving performance.
- When you are hungry or thirsty, take a break from driving.

Remember to focus on your driving at all times. A split-second distraction behind the wheel can result in injury or even death.

- Grooming (combing hair, putting on make-up or shaving);
- Eating or drinking;
- Taking notes;
- Talking with passengers;
- Tending to children or pets;
- Adjusting the controls in your vehicle (radio, CD player or climate control);
- Visual distractions outside your vehicle, such as collisions or police activity.

Careless driving is a serious offence. Police can charge drivers with careless driving if drivers do not pay full attention to their driving. If you are convicted of careless driving, you will get six demerit points and can be fined up to $2,000 and sentenced to up to six months in jail. In some cases, your licence may be suspended for up to two years.

Emergency vehicles

Emergency vehicles (police, fire, ambulance and public utility emergency vehicles) are easily identified when responding to an emergency through their use of flashing red lights (police may also use red and blue flashing lights), a siren or bell, or alternating flashes of white light from their headlamp highbeams. Also, be aware that police, fire and ambulance services use many different types of vehicles, including bicycles, snowmobiles, all-terrain vehicles, motorcycles, buses and trucks.

Reacting to an approaching emergency vehicle

When an emergency vehicle is approaching your vehicle from any direction with its flashing red or red and blue lights, or siren or bell sounding, you are required to bring your vehicle to an immediate stop.

When bringing your vehicle to a stop, you are required to bring your vehicle as near as is practicable to the right-hand curb or edge of the roadway. When on a one-way road

Stay alert

When you see an approaching emergency vehicle with its lights or siren on, prepare to clear the way.

- React quickly but calmly. Don't slam on the brakes or pull over suddenly. Use your signals to alert other drivers you intend to pull over.
- Check your rear-view mirrors. Look in front and on both sides of your vehicle. Allow other vehicles to also pull over. Pull to the right and gradually come to a stop.
- Wait for the emergency vehicle to pass and watch for other emergency vehicles that may be responding to the same call. Check to make sure the way is clear and signal before merging back into traffic.
- Don't drive on or block the shoulder on freeways. Emergency vehicle will use the shoulder of the road if all lanes are blocked.

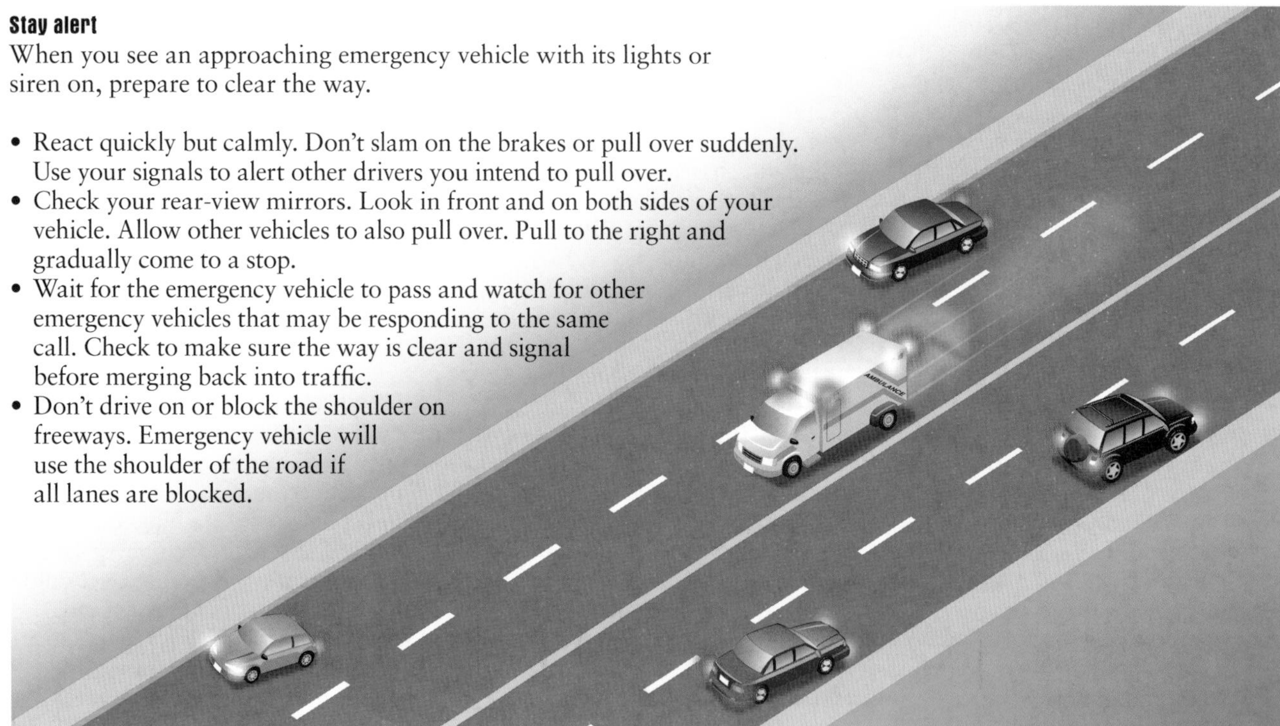

Diagram 2-46

or divided highway having more than two lanes of traffic, move to the closest curb or edge of the roadway. Your vehicle should be parallel to the roadway and clear of any intersections, including highway on/off ramps. Do not move onto or stop on the shoulder of the roadway as emergency vehicles may be travelling along it.

Use extreme caution when stopping your vehicle as other drivers may not yet be aware of or are already reacting to the approaching emergency vehicle. Look to the front, both sides and towards the rear of your vehicle, signal your intention to pull over well in advance and begin to adjust your vehicle's speed to merge with any traffic to the side you are pulling to. Once you have moved your vehicle to the side, brake gradually as required and bring your vehicle to a safe stop. Avoid any sudden changes in direction or excessive braking and be aware of any vehicles approaching fast to the rear of your vehicle.

If you are in an intersection and preparing to make a turn when an emergency vehicle is approaching, you should abandon the turn and clear the intersection by proceeding straight when safe to do so, then pull to the right and stop. This will clear the intersection and minimize the possibility of a collision with the emergency vehicle should it be passing you on the side you intended to turn towards.

When the emergency vehicle has passed, check to make sure the way is clear and signal before merging back into traffic. Remain vigilant for additional emergency vehicles and remember it is illegal to follow within 150 metres of a fire vehicle responding to an alarm.

Note: Some fire fighters and volunteer medical responders may display a flashing green light when using their own vehicles to respond to a fire or medical emergency. Please yield the right-of-way to help them respond to an emergency call quickly and safely.

Police or other enforcement officers, may require you to pull over and bring your vehicle to an immediate stop. Typically, the officer may signal this requirement by driving their vehicle with its emergency lights flashing and/or siren on behind your vehicle or by using hand gestures from the side of the road. When stopping your vehicle, follow the procedures above, except that you should bring your vehicle to a stop outside of traffic lanes and onto the shoulder of the roadway where possible, or turn and stop on a side street with less traffic if in the immediate vicinity. If the officer gives direction as to where to stop, follow the officer's directions.

Reacting to a stopped emergency vehicle

When approaching any emergency vehicle that is stopped with its red or red and blue lights flashing in the same direction of your travel, you are required to reduce the speed of your vehicle and proceed with caution. When reducing your speed, you are required to assess the speed of the surrounding traffic and the condition of the roadway (such as fog, rain, snow). To ensure safety, brake early and gradually to allow surrounding traffic to better adjust to a reduced speed and to ensure you have full control of your vehicle when braking. If your vehicle has a manual transmission, it is recommended that you use your brakes, versus shifting down to a lower gear, in order to activate your rear brake lights and indicate to other drivers that you are slowing down.

When the roadway has two or more lanes of traffic in the same direction of your travel, you are required to move into a lane away from the emergency vehicle, if safe to do so, in addition to reducing the speed of your vehicle and proceeding with caution. Similar to the procedures noted above, when slowing down and moving over, look in front and on both sides of your vehicle, and check your rear-view mirrors, to determine the speed of the traffic around you and condition of the roadway. Proceed to decrease your speed similar to surrounding traffic speed, use your turn signal prior to making the lane change, and double check your rear-view mirrors and shoulder check your blind spots to ensure no other vehicles are moving into or approaching that lane too fast. When safe to do so, change lanes well in advance of an emergency vehicle. Once in the lane, brake gradually and continue to reduce the speed of your vehicle when safe to do so. Be aware of any vehicles approaching fast to the rear of your vehicle.

Tips to remember

- Stay alert. Avoid distractions. Keep the noise level down in your vehicle.
- Remain calm, do not make sudden lane changes or brake excessively.
- Before changing direction or speed, consider road conditions, check surrounding traffic, use your mirrors, look to blind spots, and signal and brake early.
- Keep roadway shoulders, intersections and highway ramps clear for emergency vehicle use.
- If your vehicle is being pulled over, in this instance, bring it to a safe stop on the shoulder of the roadway, away from traffic, following any directions from the officer.

Failing to respond to an emergency vehicle

Take emergency flashing lights and sirens seriously. Proceed with caution, clear the way and bring your vehicle to a stop, where required. It's the law. Penalties and fines regarding reacting to an approaching or stopped emergency vehicle include:

First Offence: $400 to $2,000, plus 3 demerit points upon conviction.

Second Offence (within 5 years): $1,000 to $4,000, possible jail time up to 6 months and possible suspension of driver's licence for up to 2 years.

Chapter 2, section X — Summary

By the end of this section you should know:

- How to manoeuvre your vehicle through construction zones
- What to do if you encounter animals on the road
- Things that may distract you when driving and how to minimize those distractions
- What to do when you encounter an emergency vehicle

XI. Driving at night and in bad weather

At night and in weather conditions such as rain, snow or fog, you cannot see as far ahead, even with headlights. Slow down when driving at night, especially on unlit roads, and whenever weather conditions reduce your visibility.

Overdriving your headlights

You are overdriving your headlights when you go so fast that your stopping distance is farther than you can see with your headlights. This is a dangerous thing to do, because you may not give yourself enough room to make a safe stop. Reflective road signs can mislead you as well, making you believe you can see farther than you really can. This may cause you to over-drive your headlights if you are not careful (Diagram 2-47).

Glare

Glare is dazzling light that makes it hard for you to see and be aware what others around you are doing. It can be a problem on both sunny and overcast days, depending on the angle of the sun's rays and your surroundings. Glare can also be a problem at night when you face bright headlights or see them reflected in your rear view mirror.

When meeting oncoming vehicles with bright headlights at night, look up and beyond and slightly to the right of the oncoming lights. In daytime glare, use your sun visor or keep a pair of good quality sunglasses in your vehicle. When you enter a tunnel on a bright day, slow down to let your eyes adjust to the reduced light. Remove your sunglasses and turn on your headlights.

Cut down glare at night by following the rules of the road for vehicle lights. Use your lowbeam

Diagram 2-47

headlights within 150 metres of an oncoming vehicle or when following a vehicle within 60 metres. On country roads, switch to lowbeams when you come to a curve or hilltop so you can see oncoming headlights and won't blind oncoming drivers. If you can't see any headlights, switch back to highbeams.

Fog

Fog is a thin layer of cloud resting on the ground. Fog can reduce visibility for drivers, resulting in difficult driving conditions.

The best thing to do is to avoid driving in fog. Check weather forecasts and if there is a fog warning, delay your trip until it clears. If that is not possible or you get caught driving in fog, there are a number of safe driving tips you should follow. If visibility is decreasing rapidly, move off the road and into a safe parking area to wait for the fog to lift.

Rain

Rain makes road surfaces slippery, especially as the first drops fall. With more rain, tires make less contact with the road. If there is too much water or if you are going too fast,

Diagram 2-48

your tires may ride on top of the water, like water skis. This is called hydroplaning. When this happens, control becomes very difficult. Make sure you have good tires with deep tread, and slow down when the road is wet.

Rain also reduces visibility. Drive slowly enough to be able to stop within the distance you can see. Make sure your windshield wipers are in good condition. If your wiper blades do not clean the windshield without streaking, replace them.

In rain, try to drive on clear sections of road. Look ahead and plan your movements. Smooth steering, braking and accelerating will reduce the chance of skids. Leave more space between you and the vehicle ahead in case you have to stop. This will also help you to avoid spray from the vehicle ahead that can make it even harder to see.

Avoid driving in puddles. A puddle can hide a large pothole that could damage your vehicle or its suspension, or flatten a tire. The spray of water could obstruct the vision of adjacent motorists and result in a collision, cause harm to nearby pedestrians or drown your engine, causing it to stall. Water can also make your brakes less effective.

Flooded roads

Avoid driving on flooded roads, water may prevent your brakes from working. If you must drive through a flooded stretch of road, test your brakes afterwards to dry them out. Test your brakes when it is safe to do so by stopping quickly and firmly at 50 km/h. Make sure the vehicle stops in a straight line, without pulling to one side. The brake pedal should feel firm and secure, not spongy, that's a sign of trouble. If you still feel a pulling to one side or a spongy brake pedal even after the brakes are dry, you should take the vehicle in for repair immediately.

Tips for driving safely in fog

Before you drive — and during your trip — check weather forecasts. If there is a fog warning, delay your trip until it clears. If you are caught driving in fog, follow these safe driving tips:

DO:

- Slow down gradually and drive at a speed that suits the conditions.
- Make sure the full lighting system of your vehicle is turned on.
- Use your lowbeam headlights. Highbeams reflect off the moisture droplets in the fog, making it harder to see.
- If you have fog lights on your vehicle, use them, in addition to your lowbeams.
- Be patient. Avoid passing, changing lanes and crossing traffic.
- Use pavement markings to help guide you. Use the right edge of the road as a guide, rather than the centre line.
- Increase your following distance. You will need extra distance to brake safely.
- Look and listen for any hazards that may be ahead.
- Reduce the distractions in your vehicle. For example, turn off the cell phone. Your full attention is required.
- Watch for any electronically-operated warning signs.
- Keep looking as far ahead as possible.
- Keep your windows and mirrors clean. Use your defroster and wipers to maximize your vision.
- If the fog is too dense to continue, pull completely off the road and try to position your vehicle in a safe parking area. Turn on your emergency flashers, in addition to keeping on your lowbeam headlights.

DON'T:

- Don't stop on the travelled portion of the road. You could become the first link in a chain-reaction collision.
- Don't speed up suddenly, even if the fog seems to be clearing. You could find yourself suddenly back in fog.
- Don't speed up to pass a vehicle moving slowly or to get away from a vehicle that is following too closely.

REMEMBER:

- Watch your speed. You may be going faster than you think. If so, reduce speed gradually.
- Leave a safe braking distance between you and the vehicle ahead.
- Remain calm and patient. Don't pass other vehicles or speed up suddenly.
- Don't stop on the road. If visibility is decreasing rapidly, pull off the road into a safe parking area and wait for the fog to lift.
- Use your lowbeam lights.

Skids

A skid may happen when one or more tires lose their grip with the road's surface. Skids most often happen on a slippery surface, such as a road that is wet, icy or covered with snow, gravel or some other loose material. Most skids result from driving too fast for road conditions. Hard braking and overly-aggressive turning or accelerating can cause your vehicle to skid and possibly go out of control.

To avoid a skid on a slippery road, drive at a reduced speed and operate the vehicle's controls in a smooth and constrained manner. Increasing tire forces, such as by braking or accelerating while steering may push tires even closer to a skid condition. It's essential that the vehicle's speed be maintained at a safe level and that turns be made gently.

If your vehicle begins to skid, try not to panic — it is possible to maintain control of your vehicle, even in a skid. Ease off on the accelerator or brake and on a very slippery surface slip the transmission into neutral if you can. Continue to steer in the direction you wish to go. Be careful not to oversteer. Once you regain control you can brake as needed, but very gently and smoothly.

Anti-lock braking systems (ABS) If your vehicle is equipped with anti-lock brakes, practice emergency braking to understand how your vehicle will react. It is a good idea to practice doing this under controlled conditions with a qualified driving instructor.

ABS is designed to sense the speed of the wheels on a vehicle, during braking. An abnormal drop in wheel speed, which indicates potential wheel lock, causes the brake force to be reduced to that wheel. This is how the anti-lock braking system prevents tire skid and the accompanying loss of steering control. This improves vehicle safety during heavy brake use or when braking with poor traction.

Although anti-lock braking systems help to prevent wheel lock, you should not expect the stopping distance for your vehicle to be shortened.

Drivers unfamiliar with anti-lock braking may be surprised by the pulsations that they may feel in the brake pedal when they brake hard. Make sure you know what to expect so you will not be distracted by the pulsation or tempted to release the pedal during emergency braking manoeuvres.

Threshold braking should bring you to a reasonably quick controlled stop in your own lane, even in slippery conditions. This technique is generally practiced in a vehicle which is not equipped with ABS. Brake as hard as you can until a wheel begins to lock up, then release pressure on the pedal slightly to release the wheel. Press down on the brake pedal, applying as much braking force as possible without inducing a skid. If you feel any of the wheels begin to lock up, release the brake pressure slightly and re-apply. Don't pump the brakes. Continue braking this way until you have slowed the vehicle to the desired speed.

Vehicles equipped with ABS should provide controlled braking, on slippery surfaces automatically. Press the brake pedal hard and allow the system to control wheel lock up.

Snow

Snow may be hard-packed and slippery as ice; rutted, full of hard tracks and gullies; or, smooth and soft. Look ahead and anticipate what you must do based on the conditions. Slow down on rutted, snowy roads. Avoid sudden steering, braking or accelerating that could cause a skid.

Whiteouts

Blowing snow may create whiteouts where snow completely blocks your view of the road. When blowing snow is forecast, drive only if necessary and with extreme caution.

Tips for driving in blowing snow and whiteout conditions

Before you drive — and during your trip — check weather forecasts and road reports. If there is a weather warning, or reports of poor visibility and driving conditions, delay your trip until conditions improve, if possible. If you get caught driving in blowing snow or a whiteout, follow these safe driving tips:

DO:

- Slow down gradually and drive at a speed that suits the conditions.
- Make sure the full lighting system of your vehicle is turned on.
- Use your lowbeam headlights. Highbeams reflect off the ice particles in the snow, making it harder to see. If you have fog lights on your vehicle, use them, in addition to your lowbeams.
- Be patient. Avoid passing, changing lanes and crossing traffic.
- Increase your following distance. You will need extra space to brake safely.
- Stay alert. Keep looking as far ahead as possible.
- Reduce the distractions in your vehicle. Your full attention is required.
- Keep your windows and mirrors clean. Use defroster and wipers to maximize your vision.
- Try to get off the road when visibility is near zero. Pull into a safe parking area if possible.

DON'T:

- Don't stop on the travelled portion of the road. You could become the first link in a chain-reaction collision.
- Don't attempt to pass a vehicle moving slowly or speed up to get away from a vehicle that is following too closely.

REMEMBER:

- Watch your speed. You may be going faster than you think. If so, reduce speed gradually.
- Leave a safe braking distance between you and the vehicle ahead.
- Stay alert, remain calm and be patient.
- If visibility is decreasing rapidly, do not stop on the road. Look for an opportunity to pull off the road into a safe parking area and wait for conditions to improve.
- If you become stuck or stranded in severe weather, stay with your vehicle for warmth and safety until help arrives. Open a window slightly for ventilation. Run your motor sparingly. Use your emergency flashers.
- Be prepared and carry a winter driving survival kit that includes items such as warm clothing, non-perishable energy foods, flashlight, shovel and blanket.
- It is important to look ahead and watch for clues that indicate you need to slow down and anticipate slippery road conditions.

Ice

As temperatures drop below freezing, wet roads become icy. Sections of road in shaded areas or on bridges and overpasses freeze first. It is important to look ahead, slow down and anticipate ice. If the road ahead looks like black and shiny asphalt, be suspicious. It may be covered by a thin layer of ice known as black ice. Generally, asphalt in the winter should look gray-white in colour. If you think there may be black ice ahead, slow down and be careful.

Snow plows

Snow removal vehicles on public roadways are equipped with flashing blue lights that can be seen from 150 metres.

Flashing blue lights warn you of wide and slow-moving vehicles: some snow plows have a wing that extends as far as three metres to the right of the vehicle. On freeways, several snow plows may be staggered across the road, clearing all lanes at the same time by passing a ridge of snow from plow to plow. Do not try to pass between them. This is extremely dangerous because there is not enough room to pass safely, and the ridge of wet snow can throw your vehicle out of control.

Chapter 2, section X1 — Summary

By the end of this section you should know:

- How to identify and manage situations where your visibility may be reduced
- How weather conditions such as rain, flooded roads, snow and ice may affect your vehicle and your ability to control it
- What to do if your vehicle skids or if you encounter heavy snow, whiteouts or black ice
- How to recognize and share the road with snow removal vehicles

XII. Dealing with emergencies

If you drive often or travel alone, you need to be ready to deal with emergencies. Here are some suggestions for coping with some common road emergencies.

If your brakes fail

Try pumping the brake pedal to temporarily restore hydraulic brake pressure. If this does not work, apply the parking brake gently but firmly while holding the release button. It is a good idea for new drivers to practice a parking brake emergency stop under controlled conditions with a qualified driving instructor. Total brake failure is very rare on modern vehicles. If your brakes do fail and you manage to stop, do not drive away. Call for help.

If your gas pedal sticks

First try to lift the pedal by slipping your foot under it. Do not reach down with your hands while the vehicle is moving. If this does not work, turn on your hazard lights, shift to neutral and stop as soon as you safely can, preferably off the road. Turn off the ignition and do not drive away. Call for help.

If your headlights go out

Check the switch immediately. If the lights stay out, turn on your hazard lights and bring your vehicle to a safe stop, off the road. Call for help. It is dangerous and illegal to drive at night without lights.

If you have trouble on a freeway

At the first sign of trouble, begin to pull over. Do not wait for your vehicle to stall on the freeway. Check your mirrors, put on your hazard lights, take your foot off the gas pedal and pull over to the nearest shoulder as quickly as possible. Never stop in the driving lanes.

Be careful getting out of your vehicle. If possible, leave through the door away from traffic. If you need help, get back in the vehicle and put a “Call Police” sign in the side or back window. If you do not have a “Call Police” sign, tie a white cloth around the antenna. Do not raise the hood.

While you wait for help, stay in your vehicle with the doors locked. If someone stops to help, ask them to call the police or automobile club for you. If you have a cellular phone, call for help yourself.

The Queen Elizabeth Way, the 400-series freeways and many other high-speed roads are patrolled by the Ontario Provincial Police. Stay with your vehicle and help will arrive shortly.

If your wheels go off the pavement

Don’t panic. Grip the steering wheel firmly. Take your foot off the gas pedal to slow down. Avoid heavy braking. When the vehicle is under control, steer toward the pavement. Be prepared to correct your steering and increase speed when your wheels are fully back on the pavement.

If a tire blows out

Blowouts can cause tremendous steering and wheel vibration, but don't be alarmed. Take your foot off the gas pedal to slow down and steer the vehicle firmly in the direction you want to go. Bring the vehicle to a stop off the road.

In a collision where someone is injured

St. John Ambulance recommends that all drivers carry a well-stocked first aid kit and know how to use it. Consider reading a book about first aid or sign up for a first aid course. It could mean the difference between life and death in a collision.

Every driver involved in a collision must stay at the scene or return to it immediately and give all possible assistance. If you are not personally involved in a collision, you should stop to offer help if police or other help has not arrived.

In a collision with injuries, possible fuel leaks or serious vehicle damage, stay calm and follow these steps:

- Call for help or have someone else call. By law, you must report any collision to the police when there are injuries or damage to vehicles or other property exceeding $1,000.
- Turn off all engines and turn on emergency flashers. Set up warning signals or flares or have someone warn approaching drivers.
- Do not let anyone smoke, light a match or put flares near any vehicle in case of a fuel leak. If a vehicle is on fire, get the people out and make sure everyone is well out of the way. If there is no danger of fire or explosion, leave injured people where they are until trained medical help arrives.
- If you are trained in first aid, treat injuries in the order of urgency, within the level of your training. For example, clear the person's airway to restore breathing, give rescue breathing or stop bleeding by applying pressure with a clean cloth.
- If you are not trained in first aid, use common sense. For example, people in collisions often go into shock. Cover the person with a jacket or blanket to reduce the effects of shock.
- Stay with injured people until help arrives.
- Disabled vehicles on the road may be a danger to you and other drivers. Do what you can to make sure everyone involved in a collision is kept safe.

In a collision where no one is injured

Follow these steps in a collision where there are no injuries:

1. If the vehicles are drivable, move them as far off the road as possible as this should not affect the police officer's investigation. This is especially important on busy or high-speed roads where it may be dangerous to leave vehicles in the driving lanes. So in a minor collision with no injuries, if you can "Steer it, Clear it". If you cannot move the vehicles off the road, set up warning signals or flares far enough away to give other traffic time to slow down or stop.
2. Call police (provincial or local, depending on where the collision takes place). By law, you must report any collision to the police when there are injuries or damage to vehicles or property exceeding $1,000.
3. Give all possible help to police or anyone whose vehicle has been damaged. This includes giving police your name and address, the name and address of the registered owner of the vehicle, the vehicle plate and permit number and the liability insurance card.
4. Get the names, addresses and phone numbers of all witnesses.
5. If damage is less than $1,000, you are still required by law to exchange information with anyone whose vehicle has been damaged. However, the collision does not have to be reported to the police.
6. Contact your insurance company as soon as possible if you intend to make a claim.

Chapter 2, section XII — Summary

By the end of this section you should know:

- What to do in emergency situations such as vehicle component failure, driving off the pavement or vehicle trouble on a freeway
- The steps to take if you are involved in a collision with or without injuries

XIII. Driving efficiently

Vehicles powered by gasoline and diesel give off air pollutants and gases such as oxides of carbon, nitrogen and sulphur, hydrocarbons and soot. These pollutants affect the quality of the air we breathe, our health, crop yields and even the global climate.

Hydrocarbons and oxides of nitrogen react in sunlight to form ground level ozone, better known as smog. Smog is a major health hazard responsible for respiratory ailments and other illnesses. Oxides of sulphur and nitrogen combine with water vapour to form acid rain, which damages our lakes, forests and crops.

Global warming is the result of too much carbon dioxide and other gases trapping heat in our atmosphere. Global warming could cause average temperatures to rise, causing droughts, crop failures, lower water levels and more frequent and severe storms.

A car gives off less carbon dioxide than a larger vehicle, such as an airplane, truck, bus or train, does. However, because so many people own cars and drive them so often, cars are responsible for nearly half the carbon dioxide produced by all forms of transportation. Vehicles that carry large numbers of passengers, such as buses, produce less carbon dioxide per passenger than cars.

As a driver, you can help to protect the environment from the harmful effects of driving by following these suggestions. Many of them can also save you money.

Before you drive

- Plan ahead. Combine several errands into one trip.
- Avoid driving during rush hours. Driving in off-peak times takes less time, uses less fuel and releases fewer emissions.
- Pay attention to Smog Alerts. It is especially important to follow these suggestions on days when smog is bad.
- For short trips, consider walking or cycling.
- For longer trips, public transit is an environmentally friendly alternative to driving alone.
- Carpool whenever possible. If you want to meet at a central location, there are free carpool lots in many parts of the province. To find one near you, call MTO INFO (416) 235-4686 (1-800-268-4686) or check the MTO website at www.mto.gov.on.ca.

While driving

- Avoid starting your vehicle unnecessarily. A large burst of pollutants is emitted when a cold engine is started.
- Turn off your vehicle if parked more than 10 seconds. Even in cold weather, vehicle engines warm up within 30 seconds.
- Obey the speed limits. Driving at high speed uses more fuel

and increases your chances of a serious collision.

- On the freeway, use your vehicle's overdrive gear and cruise control for better fuel efficiency.
- Remove unnecessary weight from your vehicle, such as heavy baggage, wet snow and winter sand or salt.
- Maintain your vehicle's aerodynamics. Remove roof racks and compartments when not in use. At high speeds, use your vents instead of opening the windows.
- Use your vehicle's air conditioning wisely. Use your windows and vents in city and stop-and-go traffic. At high speeds, using your air conditioning is usually more fuel efficient than opening your windows and reducing the vehicle's aerodynamics.
- Don't 'top-off' the tank when refueling. Spilled fuel releases harmful vapours.

At the garage

- Regular maintenance will keep your vehicle running at maximum efficiency, reducing the fuel you need to buy and the pollutants your vehicle emits.
- Keep your vehicle's engine well tuned. Worn spark plugs, dragging brakes, low transmission fluid or a transmission not going into high gear can increase fuel consumption substantially.
- Follow the recommended maintenance schedule in your vehicle owner's manual to maximize fuel efficiency.
- Have any fluid leaks checked by a specialist to avoid engine damage and harming the environment.
- Keep your tires properly inflated to reduce your fuel bill, emissions and tire wear.
- Have your vehicle's alignment checked regularly to reduce uneven tire wear and fuel consumption.

(For more information on driving efficiently, see the section on maintaining your vehicle on page 139).

Chapter 2, section XIII — Summary

By the end of this section you should know:

- How passenger vehicles impact the environment
- Ways to reduce the amount you drive
- Ways to conserve fuel and reduce emissions when you drive

10 ways you can help make Ontario's roads the safest in North America

1. Don't drink and drive. Don't drive when you're taking medication that will affect your driving.
2. Always wear your seatbelt and make sure passengers are using the appropriate child car seat, booster seat or seatbelt.
3. Obey the speed limits. Slow down when road and weather conditions are poor.
4. Don't take risks: don't cut people off in traffic, make sudden lane changes or run yellow lights.
5. Don't drive when you're tired, upset or sick.
6. If you're in doubt, let the other driver go first — yield the right-of-way.
7. Keep at least a two-second space between your vehicle and the one ahead. To check your distance: start counting when the vehicle ahead passes a fixed object, stop counting when your vehicle reaches the same spot.
8. Cut the distractions: don't overcrowd the vehicle or play loud music.
9. Always check your blind spot: look in your mirror and over your shoulder before you change lanes.
10. Check traffic in all directions, including any sidewalks and paths/trails, before entering an intersection.

Choosing a driving school

As a new driver, choosing professional driving instruction may be the best way to put yourself safely in the driver's seat.

A Beginner Driver Education (BDE) course (in a driving school or high school driver education program) which has been approved by the provincial government can teach you the skills and attitudes you need to be a safe and responsible driver. The BDE course may also make you eligible to take your road test sooner and allow you to save money on insurance premiums.

As well as teaching the basics, driver training emphasizes strategic driving techniques, positive driving attitudes and behaviour, avoiding driver distractions, risk perception and management, freeway driving, night driving and driving in adverse conditions. Most programs are designed for new drivers, but many driving schools also provide courses and services to upgrade your skills.

If you graduate from an approved BDE course, the course completion information in your Driver's Licence History will reduce the time you must spend at Level 1 by four months. It may also bring you savings on your car insurance.

All ministry licenced driving schools (private or high school program) offer in-class and in-car training for a fee. All lessons are taught by a ministry-licensed driving instructor.

Ministry approved BDE courses, offered by driving schools and high schools, must last a minimum of 40 hours. This may consist of at least 20 hours in-class, 10 hours in-vehicle and 10 hours of flexible instruction that may include the following:

- Classroom Driving Instruction.
- Computer-Based Instruction.
- In-Vehicle Instruction.
- Driving Simulator Instruction.
- Homelinks (homework).

The ministry licences all driving schools offering a BDE course in Ontario. Licences are renewed every three years, if driving schools continue to meet legislative and program requirements. Only licensed instructors working for licensed schools can teach the BDE course.

All ministry-approved driving schools (i.e. schools which are licensed by the ministry) are listed on the ministry's public web-site under http://www.mto.gov.on.ca/english/dandv/driver/gradu/approve.shtml

NOTE: The ministry also lists revoked driving schools that are not on the list of approved schools, http://www.mto.gov.on.ca/english/dandv/driver/gradu/revoked.shtml

Look at the web-site for an active ministry-approved driving school that offers high quality instruction and a comfortable learning environment. Please make sure the school offers a ministry-approved BDE course of a minimum of 40 hours. The school should also be equipped with up-to-date videotapes, DVDs, Blu-Ray discs, projectors, overheads, computers, and other audio-visual aids.

- To help you choose the best driving school and course for you, please use the following checklist:
- Course information package
- Personalized program
- Adequacy of classroom facilities and related amenities
- Low student/teacher ratio
- Audio-visual equipment
- In-class topics covered
- In-vehicle topics covered
- Flexible instruction covered
- Instructor qualifications and experience
- Regular instructor upgrading
- Student progress and evaluation reports
- Minimum 20 hours classroom instruction, 10 hours behind-the-wheel instruction and 10 hours flexible instruction
- Modern training materials
- Use of vehicle for road test
- Tuition receipts
- Clear school contract statements regarding the cost of every aspect of the course including use of vehicle for road test and any subsequent road test
- Testimonials/References – history of excellent teaching, proper treatment and respect of all students with no discrimination of any type (see the Ontario Human Rights Code)
- Number of years in business
- Consumer protection insurance

Chapter 3

Traffic laws include the traffic signs and lights, pedestrian signals and pavement markings that tell drivers and other road users what they must do in certain situations. This chapter shows you what many of those signs, lights and markings look like and explains what they mean to drivers.

I. Signs

Traffic signs give you important information about the law, warn you about dangerous conditions and help you find your way. Signs use different symbols, colours and shapes for easy identification.

Here are some of the many signs you will see on Ontario roads:

A stop sign is eight-sided and has a red background with white letters. It means you must come to a complete stop. Stop at the stop line if it is marked on the pavement. If there is no stop line, stop at the crosswalk. If there is no crosswalk, stop at the edge of the sidewalk. If there is no sidewalk, stop at the edge of the intersection. Wait until the way is clear before entering the intersection.

A school zone sign is five-sided and has a yellow background with black symbols. It warns that you are coming to a school zone. Slow down, drive with extra caution and watch for children.

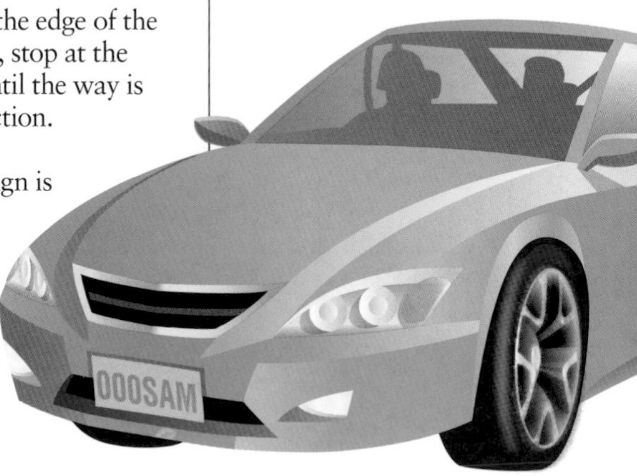

A yield sign is a triangle with a white background and a red border. It means you must let traffic in the intersection or close to it go first. Stop if necessary and go only when the way is clear.

A railway crossing sign is X-shaped with a white background and red outline. It warns that railway tracks cross the road. Watch for this sign. Slow down and look both ways for trains. Be prepared to stop.

There are four other kinds of signs: regulatory, warning, temporary conditions and information and direction.

Regulatory signs

These signs give a direction that must be obeyed. They are usually rectangular or square with a white or black background and black, white or coloured letters. A sign with a green circle means you may or must do the activity shown inside the ring. A red circle with a line through it means the activity shown is not allowed.

Here are some common regulatory signs:

This road is an official bicycle route. Watch for cyclists and be prepared to share the road with them.

You may park in the area between the signs during the times posted. (Used in pairs or groups.)

Snowmobiles may use this road.

Do not enter this road.

Do not stop in the area between the signs. This means you may not stop your vehicle in this area, even for a moment. (Used in pairs or groups.)

Do not stand in the area between the signs. This means you may not stop your vehicle in this area except while loading or unloading passengers. (Used in pairs or groups.)

Do not park in the area between the signs. This means you may not stop your vehicle except to load or unload passengers or merchandise. (Used in pairs or groups.)

Do not turn left at the intersection.

Do not drive through the intersection.

Do not turn to go in the opposite direction. (U-turn)

Do not turn right when facing a red light at the intersection.

Do not turn left during the times shown.

This parking space is only for vehicles displaying a valid Accessible Parking Permit.

No bicycles allowed on this road.

No pedestrians allowed on this road.

Keep to the right of the traffic island.

Speed limit changes ahead.

Do not pass on this road.

Slow traffic on multi-lane roads must keep right.

Indicates areas where the community has identified that there is a special risk to pedestrians. Traffic related offences committed within the zone are subject to increased fines.

The speed limit in this zone is lower during school hours. Observe the speed limit shown when the yellow lights are flashing.

STOP FOR SCHOOL BUS WHEN SIGNALS FLASHING

Stop for school bus when signals are flashing.

This sign is installed on multi-lane highways with no centre median divider. It informs drivers approaching from both directions that they must stop for a school bus when its signal lights are flashing.

These signs, above the road or on the pavement before an intersection, tell drivers the direction they must travel. For example: the driver in lane one must turn left; the driver in lane two must turn left or go straight ahead; and the driver in lane three must turn right.

Traffic may travel in one direction only.

This is a pedestrian crossover. Be prepared to stop and yield right-of-way to pedestrians.

This sign, above the road or on the ground, means the lane is only for two-way left turns.

This sign reserves curb area for vehicles displaying a valid Accessible Person Parking Permit picking up and dropping off passengers with disabilities.

These signs mean lanes are only for specific types of vehicles, either all the time or during certain hours. Different symbols are used for the different types of vehicles. They include: buses, taxis, vehicles with three or more people and bicycles.

Keep to the right lane except when passing on two-lane sections where climbing or passing lanes are provided.

This sign tells vehicles approaching a bus stopped at a dedicated Bus Stop to yield to the bus once the bus has signalled its intent to return to the lane.

High Occupancy Vehicle (HOV) signs

Only public vehicles such as buses, or passenger vehicles carrying a specified minimum number of passengers, may use this lane.

Vehicles cannot change lanes into or out of a high occupancy vehicle lane in this area.

Road forks to the right.

SCHOOL BUS LOADING ZONE

Marks a zone within which school buses load or unload passengers without using the red alternating lights and stop arm.

Warning signs

These signs warn of dangerous or unusual conditions ahead such as a curve, turn, dip or sideroad. They are usually diamond-shaped and have a yellow background with black letters or symbols. Here are some common warning signs:

Narrow bridge ahead.

Road branching off ahead.

Intersection ahead. The arrow shows which direction of traffic has the right-of-way.

Roundabout Ahead. Reduce Speed. The counter-clockwise arrows show the direction of vehicle traffic within the roundabout.

Drivers on the sideroad at the intersection ahead don't have a clear view of traffic.

Pavement narrows ahead.

Slight bend or curve in the road ahead.

Posted under a curve warning, this sign shows the maximum safe speed for the curve.

Sharp bend or turn in the road ahead.

Chevron (arrowhead) signs are posted in groups to guide drivers around sharp curves in the road.

Winding road ahead.

The bridge ahead lifts or swings to let boats pass.

Paved surface ends ahead.

Bicycle crossing ahead.

Stop sign ahead. Slow down.

Share the road with oncoming traffic.

Pavement is slippery when wet. Slow down and drive with caution.

Hazard close to the edge of the road. The downward lines show the side on which you may safely pass.

Divided highway begins: traffic travels in both directions on separated roads ahead. Keep to the right-hand road. Each road carries one-way traffic.

Right lane ends ahead. If you are in the right-hand lane you must merge safely with traffic in the lane to the left.

Traffic lights ahead. Slow down.

Steep hill ahead. You may need to use a lower gear.

Two roads going in the same direction are about to join into one. Drivers on both roads are equally responsible for seeing that traffic merges smoothly and safely.

Snowmobiles cross this road.

Bump or uneven pavement on the road ahead. Slow down and keep control of your vehicle.

Deer regularly cross this road; be alert for animals.

Divided highway ends: traffic travels in both directions on the same road ahead. Keep to the right-hand road.

Railway crossing ahead. Be alert for trains. This sign also shows the angle at which the railway tracks cross the road.

Truck entrance on the right side of the road ahead. If the sign shows the truck on the left, the entrance is on the left side of the road.

Underpass ahead. Take care if you are driving a tall vehicle. Sign shows how much room you have.

Sharp turn or bend in the road in the direction of the arrow. The checkerboard border warns of danger. Slow down; be careful.

Shows maximum safe speed on ramp.

Watch for pedestrians and be prepared to share the road with them.

Watch for fallen rock and be prepared to avoid a collision.

There may be water flowing over the road.

This sign warns you that you are coming to a hidden school bus stop. Slow down, drive with extra caution, watch for children and for a school bus with flashing red lights.

Indicates an upcoming bus entrance on the right and vehicles should be prepared to yield to buses entering the roadway.

Indicates an upcoming fire truck entrance on the right and vehicles should be prepared to yield to fire trucks entering the roadway.

These signs warn of a school crossing. Watch for children and follow the directions of the crossing guard or school safety patroller.

Temporary condition signs

These signs warn of unusual temporary conditions such as road work zones, diversions, detours, lane closures or traffic control people on the road. They are usually diamond-shaped with an orange background and black letters or symbols.

Here are some common temporary condition signs:

Construction work one kilometre ahead.

Road work ahead.

Survey crew working on the road ahead.

Traffic control person ahead. Drive slowly and watch for instructions.

You are entering a construction zone. Drive with extra caution and be prepared for a lower speed limit.

Temporary detour from normal traffic route.

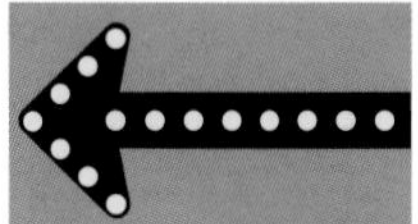

Flashing lights on the arrows show the direction to follow.

Pavement has been milled or grooved. Your vehicle's stopping ability may be affected so obey the speed limit and drive with extra caution. Motorcyclists may experience reduced traction on these surfaces.

Lane ahead is closed for roadwork. Obey the speed limit and merge with traffic in the open lane.

Closed lane. Adjust speed to merge with traffic in lane indicated by arrow.

Do not pass the pilot or pace vehicle bearing this sign.

Reduce speed and be prepared to stop.

Follow detour marker until you return to regular route.

SPEED FINES DOUBLED IN CONSTRUCTION ZONES WHEN WORKERS PRESENT

Enforces doubling the HTA fines for speeding in a designated construction zone when there are workers present.

Information and direction signs

These signs tell you about distances and destinations. They are usually rectangular with a green background and white letters. Other signs with different colours guide you to facilities, services and attractions.

Here are some common information and direction signs:

Shows directions to nearby towns and cities.

Shows the distances in kilometres to towns and cities on the road.

Various exit signs are used on freeways.

In urban areas, many exit ramps have more than one lane. Overhead and ground-mounted signs help drivers choose the correct lane to exit or stay on the freeway.

Advance signs use arrows to show which lanes lead off the freeway. Signs are also posted at the exit.

Sometimes one or more lanes may lead off the freeway. The arrows matching the exit lanes are shown on the advance sign in a yellow box with the word 'exit' under them.

Freeway interchanges or exits have numbers that correspond to the distance from the beginning of the freeway. For example, interchange number 204 on Highway 401 is 204 kilometres from Windsor, where the freeway begins. Distances can be calculated by subtracting one interchange number from another.

The term 'VIA' is used to describe the roads that must be followed to reach a destination.

Shows the upcoming roundabout exists and where they will take you.

These signs change according to traffic conditions to give drivers current information on delays and lane closures ahead.

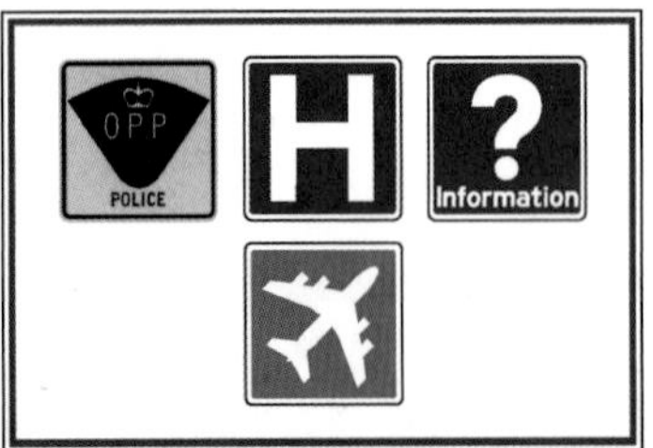

Shows off-road facilities such as hospitals, airports, universities or carpool lots.

Shows route to passenger railway station.

Shows route to airport.

Shows route to ferry service.

Shows facilities that are accessible by wheelchair.

Other signs

Here are some other common signs:

The “slow-moving vehicle” sign is an orange triangle with a red border. It alerts other drivers that the vehicle ahead will be travelling at 40 km/h or less. When on a road, farm tractors, farm implements/machinery, and vehicles not capable of sustaining speeds over 40 km/h must display the slow moving vehicle sign. Watch for these slow moving vehicles and reduce your speed as necessary.

EDR signs are used during the unscheduled closure of a provincial highway when OPP detour all traffic off the highway. The EDR markers are located along alternative routes and provide direction to motorists around the closure and back onto the highway.

Emergency response signs

Some information signs include a numbering system along the bottom of the sign to assist emergency vehicles and drivers in determining an appropriate route.

Bilingual signs

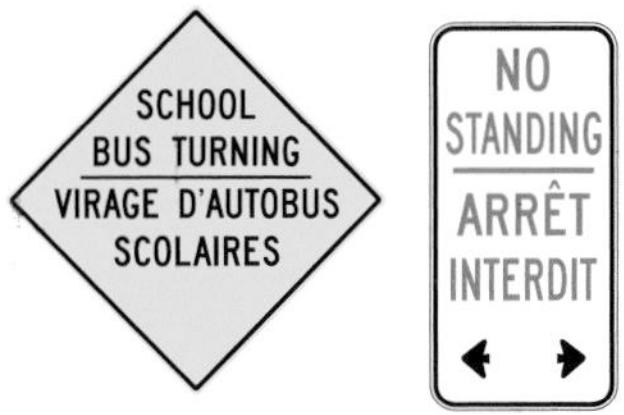

Watch for these signs when driving in designated bilingual areas. Read the messages in the language you understand best. Bilingual messages may be together on the same sign or separate, with an English sign immediately followed by a French sign.

Chapter 3, section I — Summary

By the end of this section you should know:

- The difference between regulatory, warning, temporary condition and information/direction signs
- How to read the symbols and messages of some common signs in each category

II. Traffic lights

Traffic lights tell drivers and pedestrians what they must do at intersections and along roads. They tell road users when to stop and go, when and how to turn and when to drive with extra caution.

Green light

A green light means you may turn left, go straight or turn right after yielding to vehicles and pedestrians already in the intersection. When turning left or right you must yield the right-of-way to pedestrians crossing the intersection.

Yellow light

A yellow — or amber — light means the red light is about to appear. You must stop if you can do so safely; otherwise, go with caution.

Red light

A red light means you must stop. Bring your vehicle to a complete stop at the stop line if it is marked on the pavement. If there is no stop line, stop at the crosswalk, marked or not. If there is no crosswalk, stop at the edge of the sidewalk. If there is no sidewalk, stop at the edge of the intersection.

Wait until the light changes to green and the intersection is clear before moving through it.

Unless a sign tells you not to, you may turn right on a red light only after coming to a complete stop and waiting until the way is clear. You may also turn left on a red light if you are moving from a one-way road onto a one-way road, but you must come to a complete stop first and wait until the way is clear.

Lights and arrows to help turning vehicles

Flashing green lights and green arrows direct drivers who are turning.

Advance green light or arrow

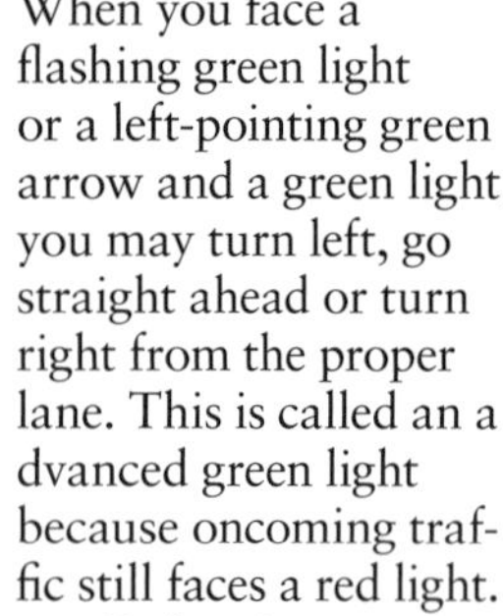

When you face a flashing green light or a left-pointing green arrow and a green light, you may turn left, go straight ahead or turn right from the proper lane. This is called an a dvanced green light because oncoming traffic still faces a red light.

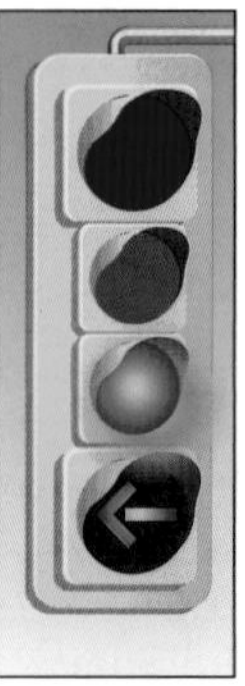

Pedestrians must not cross on a flashing green light unless a pedestrian signal tells them to.

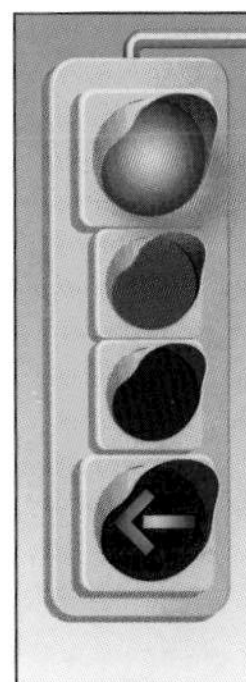

Simultaneous left turn

When a left-turn green arrow is shown with a red light, you may turn left from the left-turn lane. Vehicles turning left from the opposite direction may also be making left turns because they too face a left-turn green arrow.

After the left-turn green arrow, a yellow arrow may appear. This means the green light is about to appear for traffic in one or both directions. Do not start your left turn. Stop if you can do so safely; otherwise, complete your turn with caution.

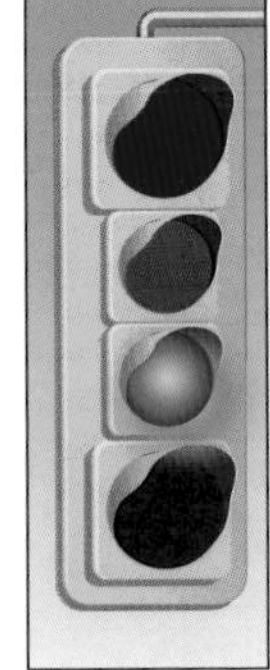

You can still turn left when the light is green, but only when the way is clear of traffic and pedestrians. If the light turns red when you are in the intersection, complete your turn when it is safe.

Pedestrians must not cross on a left-turn green arrow unless a pedestrian signal tells them to.

Transit priority signals

Traffic and pedestrians must yield to public transit vehicles at a transit priority signal. The round signal is on top of a regular traffic signal and shows a white vertical bar on a dark background. This allows transit vehicles to go through, turn right or left, while all conflicting traffic faces a red light.

Fully protected left turn

Some intersections have separate traffic lights for left-turning traffic and for traffic going through the intersection or turning right.

When a left-turn green arrow appears for traffic in the left-turn lane, traffic going straight ahead or turning right will usually see a red light. You may turn left from the left-turn lane when you face a green arrow. Vehicles from the opposite direction may also be turning left.

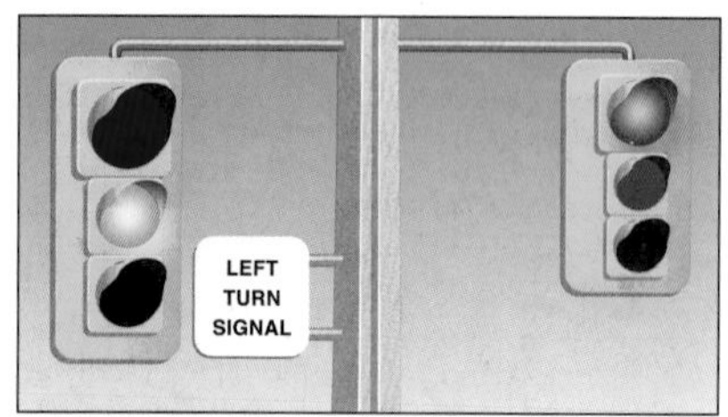

After the left-turn green arrow, a yellow light appears for left-turning vehicles only.

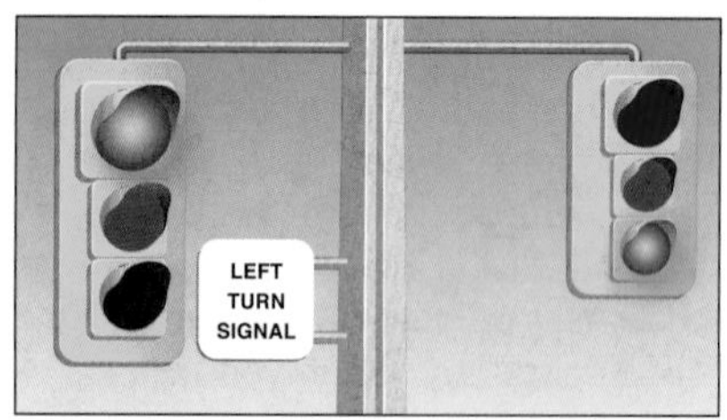

After the yellow light, a red light appears for left-turning vehicles only. Traffic going straight ahead or turning right will face a green light or green arrows pointing straight ahead and to the right.

In these intersections, you may not begin turning left after the green light appears for traffic going straight ahead or turning right. If the light turns yellow while you are in the intersection, complete your turn with caution.

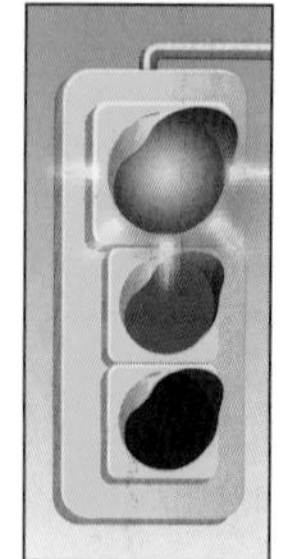

Flashing red light

You must come to a complete stop at a flashing red light. Move through the intersection only when it is safe.

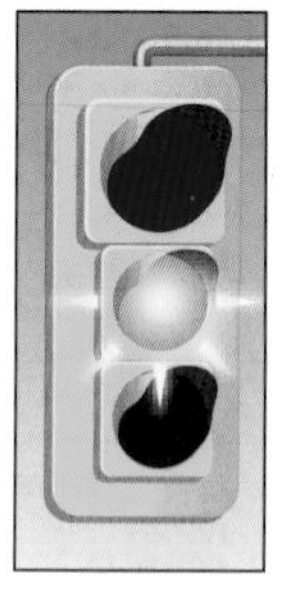

Flashing yellow light

A flashing yellow light means you should drive with caution when approaching and moving through the intersection.

Blank traffic lights

During an electrical power loss, traffic lights at intersections will not work. Yield the right-of-way to vehicles in the intersection and to vehicles entering the intersection from your right. Go cautiously and use the intersection the same way you would use an intersection with all-way stop signs.

Traffic beacons

A traffic beacon is a single flashing light hung over an intersection or placed over signs or on obstacles in the road.

Flashing red beacon

A flashing red beacon above an intersection or stop sign means you must come to a complete stop. Move through the intersection only when it is safe to do so.

Flashing yellow beacon

A flashing yellow beacon above an intersection, above a warning sign or on an obstruction in the road, warns you to drive with caution.

Chapter 3, section II — Summary

By the end of this section you should know:

- The different colours and symbols that appear on traffic lights and what those mean
- How to navigate turns using advanced green lights and arrows
- How to proceed when approaching flashing amber or red lights
- What to do in situations where the traffic lights are not operating

III. Pedestrian signals

Pedestrian signals help pedestrians cross at intersections with traffic lights. The signal for pedestrians to walk is a white walking symbol. A flashing or steady orange hand symbol means pedestrians must not begin to cross.

A pedestrian facing a walk signal may cross the road in the direction of the signal. While crossing, pedestrians have the right-of-way over all vehicles.

A pedestrian facing a flashing or steady hand symbol should not begin to cross the road. Pedestrians who have already begun to cross when the hand signal appears, should go as quickly as possible to a safe area. While they are crossing, pedestrians still have the right-of-way over vehicles.

At intersections with traffic lights where there are no pedestrian signals, pedestrians facing a green light may cross. Pedestrians may not cross on a flashing green light or a left-turn green arrow.

Intersection pedestrian signals

Where there are pedestrian push-buttons, a pedestrian must use the button to bring on the walk signal. Pedestrian signals give people more time to cross than regular traffic lights. On a busy main road, an intersection pedestrian signal helps people to cross the road safely by signalling traffic to stop. The intersection pedestrian signal has one or more crosswalks; pedestrian walk and don't walk signals; push buttons for pedestrians; and, traffic signal lights on the main road only. Stop signs control traffic on the smaller, less busy crossroad.

You must observe, obey the traffic rules and use safe driving skills to drive through these intersections. See also the section on driving through intersections on page 42.

Chapter 3, section III — Summary

By the end of this section you should know:

- What the symbols on pedestrian signals indicate
- What an intersection pedestrian signal is and what to do if you encounter one

IV. Pavement markings

Pavement markings combine with road signs and traffic lights to give you important information about the direction of traffic and where you may and may not travel. Pavement markings divide traffic lanes, show turning lanes, mark pedestrian crossings, indicate obstacles and tell you when it is not safe to pass.

Diagram 3-1
Yellow lines separate traffic travelling in opposite directions. White lines separate traffic travelling in the same direction.

Diagram 3-2
A solid line at the left of your lane means it is unsafe to pass. ('A' should not pass.)

Diagram 3-3
A broken line at the left of your lane means you may pass if the way is clear. ('A' may pass if there are enough broken lines ahead to complete the pass safely.)

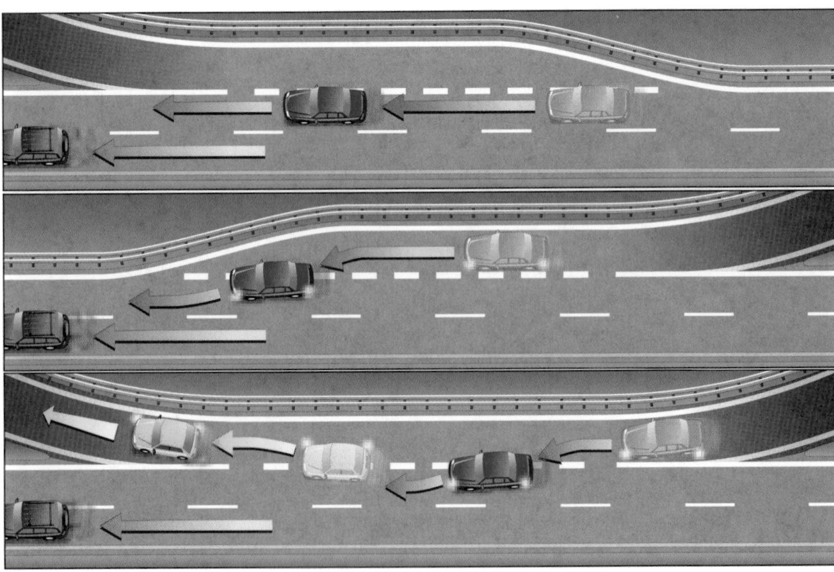

Diagram 3-4
Broken lines that are wider and closer together than regular broken lines are called continuity lines. When you see continuity lines on your left side, it generally means the lane you are in is ending or exiting and that you must change lanes if you want to continue in your current direction. Continuity lines on your right mean your lane will continue unaffected.

Diagram 3-5

A stop line is a single white line painted across the road at an intersection. It shows where you must stop. If there is no stop line marked on the road, stop at the crosswalk, marked or not. If there is no crosswalk, stop at the edge of the sidewalk. If there is no sidewalk, stop at the edge of the intersection.

Diagram 3-6

A crosswalk is marked by two parallel white lines painted across the road. However, crosswalks at intersections are not always marked. If there is no stop line, stop at the crosswalk. If there is no crosswalk, stop at the edge of the sidewalk. If there is no sidewalk, stop at the edge of the intersection.

Diagram 3-7

A white arrow painted on a lane means you may move only in the direction of the arrow.

Diagram 3-8

A pedestrian crossover is marked by two white double parallel lines across the road with an X in each lane approaching it, and overhead yellow lights. Stop before the line and yield to pedestrians.

Diagram 3-9

Two solid lines painted on the pavement guide traffic away from fixed objects such as bridge piers or concrete islands. Yellow and black markings are also painted on the objects themselves as warnings.

Chapter 3, section IV — Summary

By the end of this section you should know:

- How pavement markings are used to control traffic
- What the different colours and types of markings are used to indicate

Chapter 4

KEEPING YOUR DRIVER'S LICENCE

Ontario has a one-piece driver's licence. The licence card has a photograph and signature of the driver. All drivers in Ontario should have a one-piece licence card.

You must carry your licence with you whenever you drive.

Renewing your licence

You will get a renewal application form in the mail. Take the form into any Driver and Vehicle Licence Issuing Office in the province. They are all equipped to take photographs. You will be asked to sign the form, show identification, pay a fee and have your photograph taken. You will get a temporary licence on the spot if your application and documents are in order, and your permanent one will be mailed to you. You must carry it with you whenever you drive and produce it when a police officer requests it.

If you do not get a renewal application form in the mail when your licence is due for renewal, call the Ministry of Transportation. You are responsible for making sure you have a valid driver's licence. You can renew an expired car or motorcycle driver's licence within one year without taking any tests.

If your licence has been suspended, cancelled or expired for more than three years, you will be required to reapply for a licence in Ontario and meet all the requirements of graduated licensing, including passing all the required tests.

Senior drivers age 80 or older

Licensing

If you are 80 years of age or older, you are required to renew your driver's licence every two years. This renewal process helps keep seniors mobile and independent longer, while helping to ensure that unsafe drivers are identified and appropriate actions are taken.

The renewal consists of a vision and knowledge test and a Group Education Session. You will be notified by mail about your licence renewal. To set up an appointment for your vision and knowledge test and the Group Education Session, call the number for your MTO regional office that appears on your renewal notice.

You may also be asked to take a road test if there is a chance you may pose a safety risk. There is no charge for any of the licence renewal requirements. You only have to pay the licence renewal fee.

More information that specifically addresses the concerns of senior drivers can be found at the Driver Licensing section of MTO's website at www.mto.gov.on.ca. You can also call the Driver and Vehicle Licensing Contact Centre at (416) 235-2999 or 1-800-387-3445.

How aging affects driving safety

- Reduced vision — especially at night;
- Difficulty judging distance and speed;
- Limited movement and range of motion;
- Slower reaction time;
- Difficulty focusing attention for long periods of time;
- Easily distracted;
- More time needed to understand what you see and hear;
- More use of prescription and/or over-the-counter drugs that may impair your driving ability.

What you can do to make your driving safer

Your health is a key factor in your ability to drive. To help you handle the demands of safe driving:

- Check with your doctor or pharmacist to make sure current and new medications will not negatively affect your ability to drive. Over-the-counter drugs and combinations of drugs can also impair your driving.
- Report to your doctor:
  - vision changes, unexplained dizziness or fainting spells;
  - frequent, chronic or severe pain.
- Avoid driving if you're experiencing pain. It can decrease your ability to concentrate and limit your movement behind the wheel.
- Have your hearing and eyes checked regularly. Peripheral vision and depth perception tend to decline over the years.

- Your doctor can recommend an exercise program to improve flexibility and maintain strength, which can help your ability to drive safely.
- Consider taking a driver's course to refresh your knowledge of the rules of the road and safe driving practices.

Ask yourself: How's my driving?

Take this test and ask yourself these questions:

- Am I experiencing an increasing number of near collisions?
- Have I been directly involved in minor collisions?
- Do I have difficulty driving through intersections, judging distance or seeing pedestrians, road signs or other vehicles?
- Do I have difficulty concentrating while driving?
- Do I get lost or disoriented on familiar roads?
- Do I have difficulty coordinating hand and foot movements?
- Am I experiencing vision problems, especially at night?
- Do I get nervous behind the wheel?
- Do other motorists frequently honk at me?
- Do family members express concern about my driving ability?
- How important is driving to me?

Your answers to these questions can help you decide whether to continue to drive, cut back to certain times such as daylight hours, or stop driving altogether. If you have checked one or more of the warning signs and are concerned about your driving ability, talk to your doctor or family and get their opinions.

At the group education session, you will learn more about these topics on senior driver safety.

Graduated licensing requalification

Under graduated licensing, novice drivers (Class G1, G2, M1and M2) progress through a two-step licensing process by completing the mandatory time periods for each level and passing the required road tests. Except for Class M1, novice drivers have five years to complete the graduated licensing process. However, if your Class G1, G2 or M2 licence is about to expire and you have not completed the process, you can regain or retain the same class of licence by passing a test and paying the five-year licensing fee. This is called 'requalification.' A notice is sent to Class G1, G2 and M2 drivers before their licence expiry date to inform them of their options. If you do not complete the graduated licensing process or requalify before your G1, G2 or M2 licence expires, you will not have a licence to drive and you must reapply for a Level One licence.

Changing your name or address

You must tell the Ministry of Transportation within six days of changing your name or address.

You will need a new licence when you change your address. You can change your address on the ServiceOntario website at www.serviceontario.ca or you can take the change of information to a Driver and Vehicle Licence Issuing Office, or mail it to the Ministry of Transportation, P.O. Box 9200, Kingston, ON, K7L 5K4. The ministry will send you a new licence. When you get it, destroy your old licence and carry the new one with you whenever you drive.

When your name changes, you need a new licence. Take the documents you must show (see the chart on this page) and your current licence to a Driver and Vehicle Licence Issuing Office. A new photograph will be taken. You will get a temporary licence to use until your permanent licence is mailed to you. Carry it with you whenever you drive.

There is no charge for getting a new licence because you change your name or address.

The chart on this page shows the documents you will need to change the name on your driver's licence.

Driver's licence laws

It is illegal to:

- Lend your licence;
- Let someone else use it;
- Use an altered licence;
- Use another licence as your own;
- Have more than one Ontario driver's licence;
- Use a fictitious or imitation licence.

Reason For Name Change	Documentation Required
Marriage	Government Issued Marriage Certificate Change of Name Certificate
Common Law Alliance	Change of Name Certificate
Adoption	Court Order for Adoption Change of Name Certificate
Under the Change of Name Act	Change of Name Certificate

The demerit point system

The demerit point system encourages drivers to improve their behaviour and protects people from drivers who abuse the privilege of driving. Drivers convicted of driving-related offences have demerit points recorded on their records. Demerit points stay on your record for two years from the date of the offence. If you accumulate too many demerit points, your driver's licence can be suspended.

New drivers — Demerit Point System for Level One and Level Two Drivers

2 or more points

You will receive a warning letter.

6 points

You may have to attend an interview to discuss your record and give reasons why your licence should not be suspended. If you do not go to the interview, your licence may be suspended.

9 or more points

Your licence will be suspended for 60 days from the date you surrender it to the Ministry of Transportation. You can lose your licence for up to two years if you fail to surrender your licence. After the suspension, the number of points on your record will be reduced to four. Any extra points could again bring you to the interview level. If you reach nine points again, your licence may be suspended for six months.

As a Level One or Level Two driver, you will have your licence suspended if you accumulate nine or more demerit points during a two-year period.

Note: If you are a novice driver and are convicted of violating any novice condition, an offence that is associated with 4 or more demerit points or receive a court-ordered suspension for an offence that would have resulted in 4 or more demerit points, you will receive the appropriate penalty and Novice Driver Escalating Sanction licence suspension. However, the demerit points will be recorded as zero on your record, and will not be counted towards the accumulated demerit point system.

Fully licensed drivers — Demerit Point System for Fully Licensed Drivers

6 points

You will receive a warning letter recommending that you improve your driving skills.

9 points

You may have to go to an interview to discuss your record and give reasons why your licence should not be suspended. You may also have to complete a driver re-examination. If you fail this test, your licence can be cancelled. If

Table of offences

you fail to attend an interview, or fail to give good reasons for keeping your licence, your licence may be suspended.

15 points

Your licence will be suspended for 30 days from the date you hand over your licence to the Ministry of Transportation. You can lose your licence for up to two years if you fail to surrender it.
After the suspension, the number of points on your driver's record will be reduced to seven. Any extra points could again bring you to the interview level. If you reach 15 points again, your licence will be suspended for six months.

Here are the demerit points for driving offences.

7 points
- Failing to remain at the scene of a collision
- Failing to stop for police

6 points
- Careless driving
- Racing
- Exceeding the speed limit by 50 km/h or more
- Failing to stop for a school bus

5 points
- Driver of bus failing to stop at unprotected railway crossing

4 points
- Exceeding the speed limit by 30 to 49 km/h
- Following too closely

3 points
- Exceeding the speed limit by 16 to 29 km/h
- Driving through, around or under a railway crossing barrier
- Failing to yield the right-of-way
- Failing to obey a stop sign, traffic light or railway crossing signal
- Failing to obey traffic control stop sign
- Failing to obey traffic control slow sign
- Failing to obey school crossing stop sign
- Failing to obey the directions of a police officer
- Driving the wrong way on a divided road
- Failing to report a collision to a police officer
- Improper driving where road is divided into lanes
- Crowding the driver's seat
- Going the wrong way on a one-way road

- Driving or operating a vehicle on a closed road
- Crossing a divided road where no proper crossing is provided
- Failing to slow and carefully pass a stopped emergency vehicle
- Failing to stop at a pedestrian crossing
- Failing to move, where possible, into another lane when passing a stopped emergency vehicle
- Driving a vehicle that is equipped with or carrying a speed measuring warning device (such as a radar detector)
- Improper use of a high occupancy vehicle (HOV) lane

2 points

- Failing to lower headlight beam
- Improper opening of a vehicle door
- Prohibited turns
- Towing people — on toboggans, bicycles, skis, for example
- Failing to obey signs
- Failing to share the road
- Improper right turn
- Improper left turn
- Failing to signal
- Unnecessary slow driving
- Reversing on a highway
- Driver failing to wear a seatbelt
- Driver failing to ensure infant passenger is secured
- Driver failing to ensure toddler passenger is secured
- Driver failing to ensure child is secured
- Driver failing to ensure passenger under 16 years is wearing seatbelt
- Driver failing to ensure passenger under 16 years is occupying a position with a seatbelt

Other ways to lose your licence

Your licence may also be suspended for the following reasons:

Escalating sanctions

Escalating sanctions for novice drivers would apply if any of the following occurrences have taken place within a 5-year period:

- Any combination of repeat violations of G1/G2/M1/M2 restrictions;
- Convictions for individual HTA offences carrying four or more demerit points; or,
- Court ordered licence suspensions for HTA convictions that would have otherwise resulted in four or more demerit points.

Escalating sanctions for hybrid drivers would apply if there is any combination of repeat violations of their novice licence (G1/G2/M1/M2) conditions within a 5-year period.

The penalties under escalating sanctions for novice and hybrid drivers are:

- 30-day licence suspension for the first occurrence;
- 90-day licence suspension for the second occurrence; and
- Licence cancellation and a requirement to re-apply for a G1/M1 after the third occurrence. Any fees paid, credit received for time spent in the program or BDE credit would be forfeited when the licence is cancelled. Please note that in the case of a hybrid driver, only the novice class licence is cancelled on the third occasion, their full class licence is maintained.

A reinstatement fee is also imposed on first and second occurrence drivers.

Zero Blood Alcohol Concentration (BAC) for novice and young drivers

All drivers who are 21 years and under, regardless of licence class, must have a BAC level of zero when operating a motor vehicle.

If you are a novice driver and are caught with any amount of alcohol in your blood, you will receive an immediate 24-hour roadside driver licence suspension and, if convicted, could face a fine up to $500 and receive at least a 30-day licence suspension under the novice driver escalating sanctions program.

If you are a fully licensed driver who is 21 years and under and you are caught with alcohol in your blood, you will receive a 24-hour roadside driver licence suspension. If convicted, you could face a fine and a 30-day licence suspension.

Medical suspension

By law, all doctors must report the names and addresses of everyone 16 years or older who has a condition that may affect their ability to drive safely. For example, addiction to alcohol or drugs are conditions that affect your ability to drive. Doctors report this information to the Ministry of Transportation and it is not given to anyone else. Your driver's licence may be suspended until new medical evidence shows that the condition does not pose a safety risk.

Discretionary HTA suspensions

Your licence **may** be suspended by court order following conviction for the following:

- If you don't tell the truth
  - in an application, declaration, affidavit or paper required by the Highway Traffic Act, its Regulations or the Ministry of Transportation.

- about vehicle liability insurance.
- If you fail to insure your vehicle.
- If you are convicted of some driving offences, included careless driving and driving 50 km/h or more over the speed limit.
- If you repeatedly travel at 50km/h or more over the speed limit.

Drivers can be suspended for up to 30 days for a first offence, up to 60 days for a second offence, and up to one year for a third or subsequent offence within a five-year period.

Mandatory HTA suspensions

Your licence **will** be suspended:

- If you are convicted of failing to stop for a police officer and the court believes you wilfully avoided police during pursuit — that you tried to escape the police. (This is a *Criminal Code* offence. Your licence will be suspended for a minimum of five years.)
- If you don't pay a traffic fine when ordered by the court.

Administrative driver's licence suspension (ADLS)

Your licence will be suspended **immediately** for 90 days:

- If your blood alcohol concentration (BAC) is more than 80 milligrams in 100 millilitres of blood (.08).
- If you fail or refuse to give a breath, blood, oral fluid or urine sample when asked by police.
- If you fail or refuse to perform physical co-ordination tests or to submit to a drug evaluation when required by police.

This suspension takes effect while you are still at the roadside or at the police station. It is an administrative suspension and is separate from any criminal charges or prosecution that may also take place. An administrative monetary penalty is also imposed on drivers who receive an ADLS.

"Warn Range" suspension

Drivers who register a blood alcohol concentration in the "warn range" of .05 to .08 pose an immediate danger to themselves and other road users. If caught driving in the "warn range", you will receive an **immediate** driver's licence suspension at the roadside:

- For 3 days for a first occurrence.
- For 7 days for a second occurrence and you must undergo a remedial alcohol education program.
- For 30 days for a third or subsequent occurrence in a five-year period and you must undergo a remedial alcohol treatment program and have an ignition interlock condition placed on your licence for 6 months. If you choose not to install an ignition interlock device, you must not drive until the condition is removed from your licence.

An administrative monetary penalty is also imposed on drivers suspended for registering in the warn range.

Novice driver violations

Drivers holding G1, G2, M1 or M2 licences must follow the specific rules for their class of licence. If you violate any of the graduated licensing conditions for your class of licence, your licence will be suspended for 30 days. This suspension takes effect from the time you surrender your licence on or after the date of the suspension. You can lose your licence for up to two years if you fail to hand over your licence.

Your licence will be cancelled:

- If you fail a driver's re-examination.
- If you don't pay your reinstatement fee or administrative monetary penalty following a suspension.
- If your cheque for licence fees is not honoured by your bank.
- If you voluntarily surrender your driver's licence to the Ministry of Transportation or it is surrendered or returned by another jurisdiction.

Criminal Code suspensions

You will receive a one-year licence suspension the first time you are convicted of a *Criminal Code* offence.

If you are convicted of a second *Criminal Code* offence, your licence will be suspended for three years. A third *Criminal Code* offence will get you a lifetime suspension from driving with the possibility of reinstatement after 10 years only if you fulfill certain requirements. Fourth time offenders convicted of a *Criminal Code* offence are suspended from driving for life with no possibility of reinstatement.

Convictions will remain on your driver's record for a minimum of 10 years. The court can order a longer suspension if it believes that keeping you off the road will improve safety.

Your licence will be suspended if you are convicted of any of the following *Criminal Code* offences:

- Driving or having care and control of a vehicle while your ability is impaired by alcohol or drugs;
- Refusing to submit to a breath test for alcohol;
- Failing or refusing to provide a breath sample for roadside testing;
- Driving or having care and control of a vehicle when your blood alcohol concentration is more than 80 milligrams per 100 millilitres of blood (.08);
- Driving or having care and control of a boat, motorized or not, when your blood alcohol concentration is more than 80 milligrams per 100 millilitres of blood (.08);
- Failing to remain at the scene of a collision to escape criminal or civil liability;

- Dangerous driving;
- Causing bodily harm by criminal negligence;
- Causing death by criminal negligence;
- Failing to stop for police.

Remedial measures

There are several types of remedial measures. The mandatory Back on Track program is for all drivers convicted of impaired driving-related *Criminal Code* offences. For drivers who repeatedly blow in the warn range of .05 to .08, there is a mandatory alcohol education for a second suspension which must be completed within 120 days of the suspension or an alcohol treatment program for a third or subsequent suspension which must be completed within 180 days of the suspension. A Driver Improvement interview is required for drivers convicted of non-impaired driving-related *Criminal Code* offences. If your driver's licence has been suspended because of a *Criminal Code* conviction, your licence will remain suspended until you have completed the remedial requirements.

Driving under suspension

You may not drive, under any circumstances, when your licence is suspended. If you are convicted of driving while your licence is suspended for an HTA offence, you will have to pay a fine of $1,000 to $5,000 for a first offence and $2,000 to $5,000 for a 'subsequent' offence. (A 'subsequent' offence is when you are convicted again within five years.) The court can order you to spend up to six months in jail, or you may have to pay a fine or do both. Six months will be added to your current suspension as well.

If you are found guilty of driving while your licence is suspended for a *Criminal Code* offence, you face a fine of $5,000 to $25,000 for a first offence and $10,000 to $50,000 for a subsequent offence within five years. You also face an additional suspension (one year for a first offence; two years for a subsequent offence) under the HTA and up to two years in prison and a three-year licence suspension under the *Criminal Code*.

Driving while prohibited

This is a prohibition order under the *Criminal Code* conviction. When convicted of violation of the order, you will get a suspension of one year for a first offence or two years for a subsequent offence. Courts can order longer prohibition, which will be matched in length by a suspension under the Highway Traffic Act.

Note: Suspended drivers must pay $150 to have their licence reinstated. This fee does not apply to reinstatement following a medical or administrative suspension of your driver's licence.

Vehicle Impoundment Program

To counter the dangerous behaviours of impaired and suspended driving, Ontario law includes seven-day vehicle impoundments for:

- Drivers operating a vehicle while under a Highway Traffic Act (HTA) licence suspension (excluding suspensions for defaulted fines or medical conditions);
- Drivers required to have a vehicle ignition interlock device and are caught driving without such a device; and,
- All drivers caught with a blood alcohol concentration (BAC) over 0.08 or who fail/refuse to comply with a demand made by a police officer under the Criminal Code of Canada (CCC).

If you are caught driving while your licence is suspended for a *Criminal Code* offence, the vehicle you are driving will be impounded for a minimum of 45 days. These vehicle impoundments apply regardless of whether the vehicle is borrowed from a friend or family member, used for business or employment purposes, rented or leased. The owner of the vehicle must pay the towing and storage costs before the vehicle will be released. This program applies to all motor vehicles including passenger vehicles, motorcycles, trucks and buses.

The Vehicle Impoundment Program makes vehicle owners responsible for ensuring that anyone driving their vehicles is not suspended. People loaning or renting their vehicles can verify that a driver's licence is valid by phone at 1-900-565-6555 or online at www.mto.gov.on.ca. You can also get a driver's abstract at Driver and Vehicle Licence Issuing Offices or ServiceOntario Kiosks. There is a nominal fee for each licence checked.

Impaired driving

Impaired driving, which means driving when your ability is affected by alcohol or a drug, is a crime in Canada. Your vehicle does not even have to be moving; you can be charged if you are impaired behind the wheel, even if you have not started to drive.

Alcohol

The police can stop any driver to determine if alcohol or drug testing is required. They may also do roadside spot checks. When stopped by the police, you may be told to blow into a machine that tests your breath for alcohol, a roadside screening device, or perform physical co-ordination tests. If you fail or refuse to provide a breath sample or to perform the physical co-ordination tests, you will be charged under the *Criminal Code.*

If you cannot give a breath sample or it is impracticable to obtain a sample of breath, the police officer can require you to provide a blood sample instead.

If the police believe that a driver is impaired because of the consumption of a drug or a combination of alcohol and a drug, the police can also require a driver to submit to a drug evaluation and then require a driver to provide blood, oral fluid or urine samples. If you fail or refuse to comply with any of these demands, you will be charged under the *Criminal Code.*

Driving impaired or with more than 80 milligrams of alcohol in 100 millilitres of blood (.08) is an offence under the *Criminal Code.* Even if your blood alcohol concentration is less than .08, you can still be charged with impaired driving under the *Criminal Code.*

You will receive an **immediate** 90-day Administrative Driver's Licence Suspension if your blood alcohol concentration (BAC) is more than .08 or if you fail or refuse to provide a breath or bodily fluid sample, perform a physical co-ordination test or submit to an evaluation. You will also be subject to an **immediate** seven-day vehicle impoundment.

If you register a BAC from .05 to .08 (known as the "warn range") you will receive an **immediate** driver's licence suspension. For a first occurrence, you will be suspended for 3 days. For a second occurrence in a five-year period, you will be immediately suspended for 7 days and you must undergo a remedial alcohol education program. For a third or subsequent time in a five year period, you will be immediately suspended for 30 days and you must undergo a remedial alcohol treatment program and have an ignition interlock condition placed on your licence for 6 months. If you choose not to install an ignition interlock device, you must not drive until the condition is removed from your licence. If there is no one else available to drive and no safe place to park your vehicle, it will be towed at your expense.

If you are 21 years of age and under and hold a full class driver's licence you must not drive if you have been drinking alcohol. Your blood alcohol level must be zero. If you are caught driving with alcohol in your blood, you will receive an immediate driver's licence suspension at the roadside for 24 hours and, if convicted, you will face a fine of up to $500 and a 30-day licence suspension.

Drivers of all ages in either Level One or Level Two of Ontario's graduated licensing system must also have a blood alcohol level of zero when driving. New drivers caught drinking and driving will receive an immediate driver's licence suspension at the roadside for 24 hours and, if convicted, will face a fine of up to $500 and will receive a suspension period as per the Novice Driver Escalating Sanctions scheme. For the first occurrence, you will be suspended for 30 days. For the second occurrence, in a five-year period, you be suspended for 90 days. For the third occurrence in a five-year period, the novice portion of your driver's licence will be cancelled and you must reapply for a G1 licence.

Novice drivers will also be charged under the *Criminal Code* if their BAC exceeds .08 and will be issued a warn range suspension if they register a BAC from .05 to .08.

Drugs

Any drug that changes your mood or the way you see and feel about the world around you will affect the way you drive. *Criminal Code* and HTA sanctions apply to drivers impaired by alcohol or a drug.

In circumstances involving possible impairment by drugs or a combination of alcohol and a drug, police can require a driver to perform physical co-ordination tests and to submit to a drug evaluation and then require a driver to provide blood, oral fluid or urine samples. If you fail or refuse to comply with any of these demands, you will be charged under the *Criminal Code*. You will also receive an **immediate** 90-day Administrative Driver's Licence Suspension, and be subject to an **immediate** seven-day vehicle impoundment.

Illegal drugs such as marijuana and cocaine are not the only problem. Some drugs that your doctor may prescribe for you and some over-the-counter drugs can also impair your driving. Here are some points you should remember:

- If you use prescription medicines or get allergy shots, ask your doctor about side effects such as dizziness, blurred vision, nausea or drowsiness that could affect your driving.
- Read the information on the package of any over-the-counter medicine you take. Any stimulant, diet pill, tranquillizer or sedative may affect your driving. Even allergy and cold remedies may have ingredients that could affect your driving.
- Drugs and any amount of alcohol together can have dangerous effects, even several days after you have taken the drug. Do not take a chance, ask your doctor or pharmacist.

Consider the consequences of impaired driving

Ontario leads the way in combating drinking and driving through some of the toughest laws and programs in North America, including licence suspensions, heavy fines, vehicle impoundment, mandatory alcohol education and treatment programs and the ignition interlock program. Depending on your number of prior convictions, you may be fined up to $50,000, serve time in jail or lose your licence permanently.

For impaired driving that causes injury or death, the penalties are even more severe. If you are convicted of impaired driving causing bodily harm, you may be sentenced to up to 14 years in prison. Impaired driving causing death can carry a sentence of imprisonment for life.

If you drink and drive and are involved in a collision, you may suffer serious injury or cause serious injury to someone else. Your insurance company might not pay for your medical or rehabilitation costs, or for the damage to your or the other person's vehicle and your insurance costs may rise significantly. You may have to pay substantial legal costs as well.

If you are required to drive on the job, a licence suspension could mean losing your job.

Mandatory alcohol education and treatment

If you are convicted of an impaired driving-related *Criminal Code* offence, you must complete an alcohol education and treatment program during your licence suspension, also referred to as a remedial measures program.

If you are convicted of a drinking and driving related *Criminal Code* offence, you must take the impaired driving program called Back on Track, delivered by the Centre for Addiction and Mental Health. The three-part program, which is available across the province, involves assessment, education or treatment, and follow-up. You must pay for the program. If you have not completed the Back on Track program by the time your *Criminal Code* suspension expires, your licence will be further suspended until you have completed the remedial requirements.

This program also applies to Ontario residents convicted of driving-related *Criminal Code* offences in any other province of Canada, or equivalent offences in the states of Michigan and New York, as well as to out-of-province drivers who are convicted in Ontario.

If your driver's licence has been suspended for driving in the warn range of .05 to .08 for a second time in a five-year period you must complete a remedial alcohol education program in 120 days from the date of the suspension. For a third or subsequent occurrence of driving in the warn range, you must complete a remedial alcohol treatment program within 180 days from the date of the suspension. You must pay for these remedial programs which are also delivered by the Centre for Addiction and Mental Health. Failure to complete the required remedial program within the specified time period will result in a licence suspension until the remedial program is completed.

Driver improvement interview

The other remedial measures program is for drivers convicted of non-drinking and driving related *Criminal Code* offences who have no previous alcohol-related convictions. You must undergo a Ministry of Transportation driver improvement interview.

If you have not completed the driver improvement interview by the time your *Criminal Code* suspension expires, your licence will be further suspended until you have completed the remedial requirements.

This program also applies to Ontario residents convicted of driving-related *Criminal Code* offences in any other province of Canada, or equivalent offences in the states of Michigan and New York, as well as to out-of-province drivers who are convicted in Ontario.

Ignition interlock

An ignition interlock device is an in-car breath screening device. It prevents a vehicle from starting if it detects a blood alcohol concentration over a pre-set limit of 20 milligrams of alcohol per 100 millilitres of blood (.02).

If you are convicted of an impaired driving offence under the *Criminal Code* of Canada, after serving a licence suspension, completing a mandatory remedial measures program and meeting all licensing conditions, you will be eligible to have your driver's licence back. At that time, an ignition interlock condition is placed on your Ontario driver's licence, which means that you must install an ignition interlock device in your vehicle.

If you choose not to install a device, you must not drive until the condition is removed from your licence. Drivers caught without a required ignition interlock device will have their cars impounded for 7 days. If you are required to complete a road test while the ignition interlock condition is on your licence, you must complete a road test in a vehicle equipped with the device.

You must apply to the Ministry of Transportation to have the condition removed from your licence indefinitely. If you have completed the minimum period (one year or three years) without any program violations (tampering/driving without/missed appointment with service provider), the ignition interlock condition will be removed. If you do not apply for removal of the licence condition, it will remain on your licence indefinitely.

If it is your first conviction, you may be eligible to participate in the Reduced Suspension with Ignition Interlock Conduct Review Program. This Program will allow eligible drivers to reduce their licence suspension in return for meeting specific requirements, such as the mandatory installation of an approved ignition interlock device in their vehicle.

As a vehicle owner, you must not allow a person with an ignition interlock condition to drive your vehicle or you could be convicted of an offence under the Highway Traffic Act. You can find out if a driver has an ignition interlock condition on his or her licence by accessing MTO's website at www.mto.gov.on.ca or by calling 1-900-565-6555. There is a fee for each licence check.

If your driver's licence has been suspended for driving in the warn range of .05 to .08 for a third or subsequent time in a five-year period, you will also have an ignition interlock licence condition placed on your licence for 6 months. More information on the Program is available on the MTO website.

Chapter 4 — Summary

By the end of this section you should know:

- Your responsibility to maintain a valid driver's licence with the most correct and up to date information
- How the Demerit Point System works for new and fully licensed drivers
- The driving offences that result in a loss of points upon conviction.
- Common circumstances where your licence can be cancelled or suspended
- How alcohol and drugs impact your ability to drive
- The consequences that can result from a suspended licence including reinstatement fees, remedial measures, ignition interlock, vehicle impoundment and jail time

Chapter 5

YOUR VEHICLE

All motor vehicles on Ontario roads must be registered, insured and maintained to meet certain basic safety standards. If you own a vehicle, you are responsible for making sure it meets the requirements. People who buy and sell vehicles also have certain responsibilities.

I. Maintaining your vehicle

It is illegal to drive a vehicle in dangerous condition. But maintaining your vehicle also makes sense from an economic point of view: it can mean better mileage and a better price when you sell your vehicle. Maintaining your vehicle also helps to protect the environment.

A police officer or Ministry of Transportation inspector can examine your vehicle, its equipment and any trailer attached to it, at any time. If the vehicle is found to be unsafe, it may be taken off the road until the problem is fixed. If you refuse to allow the examination, you can be fined up to $1,000. If the vehicle is then found to be unsafe, your licence plates can be taken away.

The following driver habits and regular maintenance will help keep your vehicle fit and safe.

Driver habits

Driver habits are the things which you can do whenever you drive a vehicle. If you identify any concerns or deficiencies, further investigation or actions, including inspection and repair by a qualified mechanic, should be considered. The vehicle's owner manual often has detailed information on what

to look for when inspecting your vehicle and how to address minor problems.

When approaching your vehicle look for signs of:

- Fresh damage;
- Fluid leaks underneath;
- Under-inflated or flat tires;
- Ajar doors, hood, trunk and fuel door/cap;
- Unsecured loads;
- Check for ice, snow, or dirt that may interfere with vehicle lighting, steering, driver visibility, or become a hazard to other motorists should it come free from your vehicle.

From the driver's seat and before driving, look for:

- Unobstructed visibility around entire vehicle;
- Burned out or dim headlamps;
- Dashboard warning lights should illuminate during engine start then go out;
- Loose objects in the vehicle.

While driving, be alert for:

- Unusual engine or exhaust noises;
- Squeaking or grinding noises when applying the brakes;
- Dashboard warning lights coming on.

When planning an extended trip, perform more detailed vehicle checks, including:

- Windshield wipers and washer fluid level;
- Tire pressures, condition and wear;
- All lights work;
- When the engine is cold, check under the hood; oil and coolant levels, obvious defects with belts, hoses, and possible leaks. Your vehicle's owner's manual should provide more information on what to check and what to look for;
- Consider having your vehicle thoroughly inspected by a qualified mechanic.

Diagram 5-1

Regular maintenance

In order to keep your vehicle running smoothly, vehicle manufacturers often establish a schedule for regular maintenance. Scheduling of this work is normally based upon accumulated vehicle mileage or time intervals (whichever comes first). Further details may be found in the vehicle's owner's manual. Regular maintenance may include oil and filter change, other fluid checks and changes, air and fuel filter replacement, tire rotation and brake inspection. Periodically, more intensive mechanical servicing such as engine adjustments and timing belt replacement, may be required.

Winter maintenance

A well-maintained vehicle will generally start in all weather conditions. However, whenever possible, shelter your vehicle from direct contact with rain or snow when it is parked because even the best maintained vehicle can't run if the engine is soaked.

Carry emergency supplies. These should include a shovel, a bag of sand or kitty litter, booster cables, emergency flares or warning lights, a blanket and a chain for towing. Always carry extra windshield washer fluid in the winter and refill the container when necessary.

Cold weather puts extra strain on your vehicle's systems. With lights, heater, defroster and radio all working at once, batteries do not get a good charge at idle speed. If idling in traffic for long periods, shift to neutral and rev the engine gently. Have your battery checked and terminals cleaned at least twice during the winter.

Faulty exhaust systems are especially dangerous in the winter when drivers are more likely to drive with windows and vents closed. Have your exhaust checked if it sounds noisy or rattles.

Tires

The type of tires you have and the way they are made are critical for good traction, mileage and safety. Keep these points in mind when you buy or replace tires, and check your vehicle owner's manual or the tire manufacturer's guide for recommendations.

Tires must meet standards described in the Canadian Motor Vehicle Safety Act. Tires deteriorate with age, even when not in use. Aged tires have reduced traction, are more prone to cracking and may fail unexpectedly while in use. Tires should not be older than ten years of age. Some tire and vehicle manufacturers have issued recommendations for replacing tires from six years of age. Consumers are advised to check with their tire or vehicle manufacturer for specific guidance. The age of the tire

Diagram 5-2

can be determined by checking the identification number on the sidewall that begins with the letters "DOT". The last four digits represent the week and year the tire was manufactured."

- Replace tires when the tread is less than 1.5 millimetres deep or when tread wear indicators touch the road. Vehicles that weigh more than 4,500 kilograms must replace their front tires when tread is less than three millimetres deep.
- Replace tires that have bumps, bulges, knots, exposed cords or tread and sidewall cuts deep enough to expose cords.
- Any tire on a vehicle must not be smaller than the vehicle manufacturer's specified minimum size. And it must not be so large that it touches the vehicle or affects its safe operation.
- Use similar tires on all four wheels. Some combinations are illegal, including: radial-ply tires on the front and bias-ply or belted bias-ply on the rear; a mix of 50 or 60 series tires on the front with any other mixture on the rear; and a combination of types or sizes on the same axle, unless the types and sizes are equivalent by industry standards. This does not apply to a single spare tire used in an emergency.
- Any tire with the wording "not for highway use", "farm use only", "competition circuit only", "NHS", "TG", "SL" or any other words that mean the tire is not for use on the road must not be used on a vehicle that travels on a public highway.
- Winter tires or all-weather tires are not required by law. To provide the best traction during the winter season, it is recommended that your vehicle be equipped with four winter or all-weather tires with the same tread pattern. If using only two winter tires, regardless of whether the vehicle is front, rear or all wheel drive, these should be installed on the rear axle for best vehicle stability in turns and during braking.
- If you live in Northern Ontario, you can legally use studded tires on your vehicle. Research shows that studded tires are more effective than other tires under icy conditions, particularly on wet ice. Overall, winter tires perform better than conventional all season tires under all wintertime conditions.
- Scrap tires are a serious environmental concern. Proper tire maintenance will extend the life of a tire and delay its disposal. Some tips for longer wear: maintain the right air pressure; inspect tires for wear; rotate tires regularly; and practice good driving habits.

II. Vehicle insurance and registration

Insurance

Ontario has compulsory automobile insurance. This means every vehicle registered in the province must be insured.

You must show proof that you have insurance coverage before you can register a vehicle or renew your registration. If you do not tell the truth about your insurance or if you show false documents, you can be fined $5,000 to $25,000. You may also lose your driver's licence for up to one year and have your vehicle taken away for up to three months.

You must insure all your vehicles for third party liability of at least $200,000. This covers you in the event that you injure or kill someone or damage someone's property. Collision insurance to cover damage to your own vehicle is a good idea but not required by law.

When driving your own vehicle or someone else's, you must carry the pink insurance card from the insurance company for that particular vehicle. You must show this card when a police officer asks for it. If you do not, you can be fined up to $400.

Registration

Vehicle registration includes licence plates and a vehicle permit. Licence plates in Ontario are based on a plate-to-owner system. This means that vehicle licence plates move with the vehicle owner, not the vehicle. When you sell or change vehicles, you must remove your plates. If you do not intend to use them on another vehicle, you may return your plates to a Driver and Vehicle Licence Issuing Office.

Your vehicle permit must have an accurate description of your vehicle. This means that if you change your vehicle, such as the colour, you must report it at a Driver and Vehicle Licence Issuing Office within six days.

If you own a vehicle and you change your name or address, you must notify the Ministry of Transportation within six days. You can do this in person at a Driver and Vehicle Licence Issuing Office, on the ServiceOntario website at www.serviceontario.ca, or by mail, using the change of information stub attached to your vehicle permit.

New residents

New Ontario residents have 30 days to register their vehicles. To get a vehicle permit and Ontario licence plates, go to a Driver and Vehicle Licence Issuing Office. You must bring along:

- A Safety Standards Certificate;

- Proof of insurance;
- A Vehicle Import Form 1 if you have brought the vehicle in from another country;
- The vehicle permit, or ownership, from where you used to live;
- Proof of passing a Drive Clean vehicle emissions test, if a test is required. To find out if your vehicle needs one, visit www.driveclean.com or call the Drive Clean Contact Centre at 1-888-758-2999. Out-of-province callers may call 1-905-440-7482 (charges apply).

III. Buying or selling a used vehicle

If you are selling a used vehicle privately in Ontario, you must buy a Used Vehicle Information Package. This applies to the private sale of any car, van, light truck, motor home, moped, limited-speed motorcycle or motorcycle. The package is available from any ServiceOntario office or online at www.serviceontario.ca.

The package, which the seller must show to potential buyers, a description of the vehicle, its registration and lien history in Ontario and the average wholesale and retail values for its model and year. It also includes information about retail sales tax.

As well as giving the buyer the Used Vehicle Information Package, sellers must remove their licence plates, sign the vehicle transfer portion of their vehicle permit and give it to the buyer. Sellers must keep the plate portion of the permit.

The buyer must take the package and the vehicle portion of the permit to a Driver and Vehicle Licence Issuing Office to register as the new owner within six days of the sale.

Before buyers can put their own plates on their new vehicle, they must have:

- Their licence plates validated;
- The vehicle portion of the permit issued for the vehicle;
- Their own licence plate number recorded on the plate portion of the vehicle permit;
- A valid Safety Standards Certificate;
- The minimum insurance required under the Compulsory Automobile Insurance Act;
- Proof of passing a Drive Clean vehicle emissions test may be required as used vehicles usually need a Drive Clean pass to register license plates under the

new owner. However, exemptions apply. Visit the Drive Clean website at www.driveclean.com to see if your vehicle needs a test or to view the Drive Clean emissions test history of a vehicle.

Safety Standards Certificate

A Safety Standards Certificate is a document that certifies a vehicle's fitness. You can buy and register a vehicle without a safety certificate, but you cannot put your own plates on the vehicle or drive it without one. Any inspection station in Ontario licensed by the Ministry of Transportation can issue a Safety Standards Certificate, provided your vehicle passes an inspection. Many garages are licensed — look for a sign saying it is a Motor Vehicle Inspection Station.

A Safety Standards Certificate is valid for 36 days after the inspection. However, the certificate is not a guarantee or warranty that the vehicle will stay fit for any period.

Mandatory Vehicle Branding Program

Under the Mandatory Vehicle Branding Program, insurers, self-insurers (fleet owners), auctioneers, importers, salvagers and anyone who deals in used vehicles, are required to determine whether severely damaged and written off ('total loss') vehicles they insure or obtain should be branded either 'Irreparable' or 'Salvage'. They must notify the ministry of the brand through a Notification of Vehicle Brand form. The ministry applies the brand to the vehicle's registration information so that it will appear on the vehicle permit, vehicle abstracts and the Used Vehicle Information Package (UVIP) for that vehicle. The brand identifies the condition of the

vehicle to potential buyers. This is how the program helps to protect consumers buying used vehicles.

If your vehicle sustains severe damage and is written off by your insurance company, your insurance company must notify you and the ministry of the brand requirement. If you do not receive a claim settlement through an insurance company, you must have the brand determined by an authorized mechanic at a Type 6 Motor Vehicle Inspection Station. The ministry website has a list of these facilities, visit mto.gov.on.ca for details.

There are four brands:

- A vehicle which has never had a brand applied in Ontario automatically has the brand 'None' applied to its registration documents. However, this does not mean that the vehicle has never been damaged in a collision, was never branded in another jurisdiction or was not rebuilt prior to the mandatory branding program.
- The brand 'Irreparable' means that damage to the vehicle was so severe that the vehicle can be used for parts or scrap only. It cannot be rebuilt, and it can never be driven in Ontario.
- The brand 'Salvage' means that the damaged vehicle can be repaired or rebuilt. It cannot be registered as fit to drive in Ontario. Once the vehicle has been repaired or rebuilt, and if it can pass a structural inspection to ministry standards, the owner can obtain a Structural Inspection Certificate and have the vehicle branded as 'Rebuilt'.
- The brand 'Rebuilt' means that the vehicle has been previously branded as 'Salvage', but has been rebuilt and has passed a structural inspection to ministry standards. If the vehicle can pass a safety inspection (Safety Standards Certificate), the owner can have it registered as fit to drive in Ontario.

Motorcycles that have been written off must be branded 'Irreparable'; they cannot be branded 'Salvage'.

Trailers, traction engines, farm tractors, motor assisted bicycles, motorized snow vehicles, street cars or motor vehicles with a model year of 1980 or earlier are exempt from the mandatory branding program.

Ontario's Drive Clean program

Vehicles are a major domestic source of smog-causing emissions in Ontario. Drive Clean, administered by the Ministry of the Environment, reduces smog-causing pollutants from vehicles by testing them to identify emissions problems and requiring vehicles to be repaired.

Effective September 1, 2011, changes to the program exempted some vehicles from testing:

- Vehicles are tested for registration renewal at seven years of age, instead of five.
- Light-duty vehicles no longer require a test for family transfers and lease buyouts by the lessee, unless the test is normally scheduled for that year.
- No test is required for licence renewal if your light-duty vehicle passed the test in the previous calendar year.
- Vehicles plated "Historic" no longer require testing.

If your vehicle registration expired before September 1, 2011, the previous rules apply.

Light-duty Vehicles (weigh less than 4,500 kg)

Most passenger cars, vans, and light trucks registered in the southern Ontario Drive Clean area must pass a test every two years in order to renew licence plates. Visit the website for details on exemptions and the Conditional Pass.

Heavy-duty Vehicles (commercial vehicles weighing 4,500 kg or more)

Diesel trucks and buses registered anywhere in the province and non-diesel vehicles registered in the southern Ontario Drive Clean area must be tested every year and be fully repaired. An incentive is available to encourage maintenance.

For more information about Drive Clean, visit www.driveclean.com

IV. Towing

This chapter tells you what you need to know to tow a trailer behind a car, van or small truck in Ontario. This includes licence and registration requirements, trailer size and characteristics, as well as safety tips to follow when towing a trailer.

Before you attempt to tow a trailer, consider the size, power and condition of your vehicle. Make sure it is capable of towing both the trailer and the load you intend to carry, and that your trailer and hitch meet all the requirements described in this chapter.

Towing a trailer brings unique challenges to drivers. Almost half of the reported collisions while towing a recreational vehicle are single vehicle collisions. Another 20% involve rear-end collisions. In collisions where the driver was determined to be at fault, about 30% of the drivers had "lost control" of their vehicle.

Licence and permit

You must have a valid driver's licence (Class G1, G2 or G) or higher class of licence to tow a trailer with a gross vehicle weight of up to 4,600 kilograms. If your trailer and load exceeds the size and weight specified in the Highway Traffic Act, you may need a higher class of licence or an oversize vehicle permit to tow it. Oversize permits are available at some MTO Driver and Vehicle Licence Issuing Offices.

It is against the law to tow more than one trailer behind non-commercial vehicles.

Registering your trailer

A trailer is considered a separate vehicle. Before you can tow one on any public road, you must register it and pay a one-time registration fee at a Driver and Vehicle Licence Issuing Office. When you register your trailer you will receive a licence plate and vehicle permit. Attach the licence plate to the back of your trailer where it is clearly visible. Always carry your permit, or a copy of it, to show to a police officer when asked.

Make sure your trailer is in good condition

Your trailer must be in safe operating condition. If it is not, a police officer may remove your trailer from the road until it is made safe to operate.

Brakes

If your trailer has a gross trailer weight, vehicle and load of 1,360 kg or more, it must have brakes strong enough to stop and hold the trailer.

Lights

Your trailer must have:

- a white licence plate light;
- a red tail light; and,
- two red reflectors at the rear of the trailer, as far apart as possible.

If your trailer is wider than 2.05 metres, it must also have:

- two yellow clearance lights, one on each side at the front of the trailer, as far apart as possible, to let drivers coming toward you know the width of your trailer; and,
- two red clearance lights, or reflectors, one on each side at the rear of the trailer, as far apart as possible, to let drivers behind you know the width of your trailer.

Your trailer must have mudguards, fenders and flaps or be designed in such a way that it does not spray or splash traffic travelling behind you.

If the load in your trailer blocks your vision to the rear, you must have additional mirrors that provide a clear view of the road to the rear. Load your trailer carefully so that nothing comes loose or falls off while you are moving.

Attaching your trailer

Your trailer must have two separate ways of attaching to your vehicle so that if one fails or comes loose, the trailer will stay attached.

If safety chains are used, they must be crossed under the tongue to prevent the tongue from dropping to the road if the primary hitch accidentally disconnects. The chain hooks must have latches or devices that will not accidentally become detached.

No passengers

You may not carry any person in any trailer, including a house or boat trailer, when it is being towed.

Trailer hitch

Use a good quality trailer hitch. The class of trailer hitch you use depends upon the gross weight of your trailer — the gross weight being the total weight of the trailer and its load. Make sure you use the right trailer hitch for the weight of your trailer. It should be securely attached to your vehicle following manufacturer's recommendations.

The hitch-ball should be installed so that when the trailer is attached and tightened, it is level with no tilting. If the hitch pulls down the rear of your vehicle, you may need to use a load-equalizing trailer hitch. You may also be able to shift some of the load in the trailer to the rear to reduce the load on the rear of your vehicle.

In addition to a ball and hitch, be sure to use safety chains or cables strong enough to hold the trailer and load, in case the ball and hitch accidentally come apart.

Loading your trailer

When loading your trailer, strap everything down, inside, as well as outside, the trailer. It is an offence to have a load that may become dislodged or may fall off. Do not overload your trailer. Too much weight in the trailer can put a strain on your vehicle and damage your tires, wheel bearings and axle. When carrying a boat on a trailer, do not carry cargo in the boat unless your trailer is designed and equipped for the extra weight.

The distribution of the weight in your trailer is also very important. Generally, more of the trailer load should be in front of the trailer axle than behind it for proper hitch weight. About 5 to 10 per cent of the trailer's total weight should be supported on the hitch, within the weight limit marked on the hitch. Poor load balance can cause your trailer to sway or fishtail. The ball and hitch may also become separated, especially if there is too much weight in the rear of the trailer.

Heavy and improperly placed loads can pull down the rear of your vehicle, lifting the front end and affecting your steering, especially in wet and slippery conditions. It may also affect the aim of your headlights so that your low beams blind approaching drivers. The alignment of your mirrors may also be affected.

Starting out

Before each trip, check the trailer hitch, wheels, tires, lights, load distribution and load security to make sure they are safe. Check your tire pressure with the trailer

loaded while the tires are still cold. When you start to drive, accelerate carefully. Drive slowly and carefully.

Curves and turns

Stay close to the middle of your lane when taking a curve. When making a right turn, check traffic. Look in your right mirror. Signal and slow down. If the turn is sharp, move ahead until your vehicle's front wheels are well ahead of the curb before turning to the right.

When making a left turn, check traffic. Signal. Proceed slowly. When you make your turn, swing wide by driving well into the intersection before turning.

Slowing down and stopping

A sudden stop can cause your trailer to jackknife or slide sideways or the load to shift. To avoid sudden stops, increase the following distance between you and the vehicle ahead. Keep out of the fast lanes and maintain a speed that will allow you to slow down and stop smoothly in any situation.

Passing

You cannot accelerate as quickly when you are towing a trailer. You also need more space because the length of your vehicle is much longer with a trailer attached. Before you pass, make sure you have enough time and room to complete the pass. Once you have passed, allow more room before you move back to your lane. Do not cut back into the lane too soon. This can cause your trailer to sway and make it difficult to control.

Being passed

If you are holding up a line of traffic, signal, pull over and let the other vehicles pass. Fast-moving trucks and buses create a strong air disturbance behind them. If a large bus or truck passes you, the wall of wind behind it may whip your trailer to the side, pushing it out of control. When you experience this, do not brake. Carefully steer your vehicle and trailer back into position. A slight increase in speed may help.

Backing up

Back up very slowly and have someone outside the vehicle direct you. Use a series of small turns to steer. It is a good idea to practice this skill off the road in an empty parking lot until you are comfortable with your ability.

To back up to the right, steer to the left. The front end of the trailer will go left, but the rear end will go right. To back up to the left, steer to the right. The front end of the trailer will go right, but the rear end will go left.

Towing disabled vehicles

If your vehicle breaks down, you should get help from a tow truck designed to tow vehicles. If you must use another vehicle to tow, use warning signals or emergency flashers and make sure you attach the vehicles securely. Someone must sit in the disabled vehicle and use the brakes to keep the tow cable tight. If the engine cannot run, don't tow vehicles that have power braking and steering. Without the engine, braking and steering is difficult and towing may lead to a collision.

Trying to start a disabled vehicle by towing is dangerous and could damage both vehicles.

Chapter 5 — Summary

By the end of this section you should know:

- The checks that need to be performed on your vehicle: daily/weekly, at its regular servicing and for its use in the winter
- How to buy the right tires for your vehicle and how to know when they need replacing
- Your responsibility to ensure that the vehicle you are driving is properly registered and insured
- Information about buying and selling used vehicles including the Safety Standards Certificate
- Licensing requirements to properly tow a trailer or disabled vehicle
- Vehicle requirements such as brakes, lights, mirrors and trailer hitches
- The proper way to load a trailer and attach it to your vehicle
- Driving techniques for driving with a trailer attached

Test yourself — Sample knowledge test questions

The following questions will give you an idea of what to expect on the knowledge test. All knowledge tests questions follow this multiple-choice format. The answers to these sample questions are provided at the bottom of the page.

1. To get your vehicle out of a skid, you should first:
   a. Steer straight ahead.
   b. Steer in the opposite direction of the skid.
   c. Steer in the direction you want to go.
   d. Apply brakes hard.

2. When may you lend your driver's licence?
   a. In emergencies.
   b. To a person learning to drive.
   c. It is not permitted.
   d. For identification purposes.

3. What must a driver do before entering a highway from a private road or driveway?
   a. Enter or cross the highway as quickly as possible.
   b. Yield right-of-way to all vehicles approaching on the highway.
   c. Sound horn and proceed with caution.
   d. Give hand signal then take right-of-way.

4. Never change lanes in traffic without:
   a. Looking in the rear view mirror only.
   b. Giving proper signal and looking to make sure the move can be made safely.
   c. Blowing your horn and looking to the rear.
   d. Decreasing speed and giving correct signal.

5. When the driver of another vehicle is about to overtake and pass your vehicle, you must:
   a. Speed up so that passing is not necessary.
   b. Move to the left to prevent passing.
   c. Signal to the other driver not to pass.
   d. Move to the right and allow such vehicle to pass.

6. When you are deciding whether or not to make a U-turn, your first consideration should be to check:
   a. Traffic regulations.
   b. Presence of trees, fire hydrants or poles near the curb.
   c. Turning radius of your car.
   d. Height of curb.

7. It is more dangerous to drive at the maximum speed limit at night than during daytime as:
   a. Your reaction time is slower at night.
   b. You cannot see as far ahead at night.
   c. Some drivers unlawfully drive with parking lights only.
   d. The roadways are more apt to be slippery at night.

8. You should under all conditions drive at a speed which will allow you to:
   a. Stop within 150 metres (500 feet).
   b. Stop within 90 metres (300 feet).
   c. Stop within 60 metres (200 feet).
   d. Stop within a safe distance.

Answer Key: 1-c, 2-c, 3-b, 4-b, 5-d, 6-a, 7-b, 8-d

Chapter 6

THE LEVEL TWO ROAD TEST

Statistics show that new drivers of all ages are far more likely than experienced drivers to be involved in serious or fatal collisions.

To help new drivers develop better, safer driving habits, Ontario introduced graduated licensing in 1994 for all drivers applying for their first car or motorcycle licence. Graduated licensing lets you gain driving skills and experience gradually, in lower-risk environments. The two-step licensing system takes at least 20 months to complete and includes two road tests. Passing the Level Two (G2) road test gives you full Class G driving privileges.

While the Level One road test deals with basic driving skills, the Level Two road test deals with advanced knowledge and skills that are generally gained with driving experience. When you take the test, the examiner will give you directions. As you complete the driving tasks, the examiner will watch to make sure you successfully perform the actions associated with them.

The G2 road test includes a component of expressway driving. To proceed with the G2 road test, you must complete and sign a "Declaration of Highway Driving Experience" to ensure that you have sufficient expressway driving experience to complete this component. On the form you will indicates how many times in the three months before the road test you have driven on a freeway and/or on a highway with a speed limit of at least 80 km/h. You are required to indicate what was the average length of these trips (i.e. under 5 km, between 5 and 15 km, over 15 km). Freeways include: 400, 401, 402, 403, 404, 405, 406, 407, 409, 410, 416, 417, 420, 427, Queen

Elizabeth Way (QEW), Don Valley Parkway (DVP), Gardiner Expressway, E. C. Row Expressway and the Conestoga Parkway. If you do not have sufficient highway driving experience, the examiner must declare the road test "out-of-order" and cancel the test. You will lose 50% of your prepaid road test fee. In order to reschedule, you will have to pay the 50% of the road test fee lost through the out-of-order. Make sure you obtain the required highway driving experience before rescheduling your test.

To help you prepare, this chapter tells you the various tasks and actions that you will be expected to perform in your Level Two road test. This is only a guide. For more information on the driving tasks, you should review chapters 2 and 3.

I. Left and right turns

The approach

This driving task begins when the examiner tells you to make a left or right turn and ends at the point just before you enter the intersection. Make sure you take the following actions:

Traffic check

Before slowing down, look all around you. Use your rear view and side mirrors to check traffic behind you. If you change lanes, remember to check your blind spot by looking over your shoulder.

Lane

Move into the far left or far right lane as soon as the way is clear.

Signal

Turn on your signal before slowing down for the turn unless there are vehicles waiting to enter the road from sideroads or driveways between you and the intersection. Wait until you have passed these entrances so that drivers will not think you are turning before the intersection.

Speed

Steadily reduce speed as you approach the turn. In a vehicle with manual transmission, you may downshift into a lower gear as you slow down. Do not coast with your foot on the clutch pedal.

Space

While slowing down, keep at least a two to three-second distance behind the vehicle in front of you.

If stopped

You will need to do this driving task if you cannot complete your turn without stopping, either because the way is not clear or you face a stop sign or red traffic light. Remember to follow these actions:

Stop

Come to a complete stop. Do not let your vehicle roll forward or backward. When traffic conditions allow, move forward to check that the way is clear or to start the turn. If you have to stop after you have passed the stop line, do not back up.

Space

When stopped behind another vehicle at an intersection, leave enough space to pull out and pass without having to back up. Leaving this space protects you in three ways: it lets you pull around the vehicle in front if it stalls; it helps prevent you from being pushed into the vehicle ahead if you are hit from behind; and it reduces the risk of collision if the vehicle ahead rolls backward or backs up.

Stop line

If you are the first vehicle approaching an intersection with a red light or stop sign, stop behind the stop line if it is marked on the pavement. If there is no stop line, stop at the crosswalk, marked or not. If there is no crosswalk, stop at the edge of the sidewalk. If there is no sidewalk, stop at the edge of the intersection.

Wheels

When waiting to make a left turn, keep your front wheels straight. With your wheels turned left, your vehicle could be pushed into oncoming traffic. When waiting to turn right, keep the wheels straight if there is a risk of being pushed into pedestrians crossing the intersection. At a large intersection with curved sidewalks where you are turning right, angle your vehicle to follow the curb so that no other vehicle can fit between you and the curb.

Making the turn

The driving task involves your actions as you make the turn. Remember to do the following:

Traffic check

If you are stopped, waiting for a green light or for the way to be clear, keep checking traffic all around you. Just before entering the intersection, look left, ahead and right to check that the way is clear. If there is any doubt about the right-of-way, try to make eye contact with nearby drivers or pedestrians. If it is possible for another vehicle to overtake you while you are turning, check your blind spot before starting to turn. You have not properly checked traffic if another vehicle or pedestrian has the right-of-way and must take action to avoid your vehicle.

Both hands

Use both hands to turn the steering wheel throughout the turn. You are most at risk from other traffic when turning. Using both hands on the wheel gives you maximum steering control when you need it most. An exception to this is if you have a disability that prevents you from using both hands.

Gears

In a vehicle with manual transmission, do not shift gears during the turn. If you need to, you may shift gears immediately after the vehicle is moving but before it is well into the turn. You may also shift gears in an intersection wider than four lanes if not doing so would slow down other traffic. Generally, not changing gears gives you more control over your vehicle when turning.

Speed

Move ahead within four to five seconds after it is safe to start. Make the turn at a steady speed, increasing speed as you complete the turn. Drive slowly enough to keep full control of your vehicle without slowing down other traffic.

Wide/short

Turn into the corresponding lane on the intersecting road without going over any lane markings or curbs.

Completing the turn

This driving task completes the turn. It begins when you enter the intersecting road and ends when you return to normal traffic speed. Take the following actions:

Lane

End your turn in the lane that corresponds to the lane you turned from. If you are turning left onto a multi-lane road, return to normal traffic speed and move into the curb lane when it is safe to do so. If you are turning right onto a road where the right lane is blocked with parked vehicles or cannot be used for other reasons, move directly to the next available lane.

Traffic check

As you return to normal traffic speed, check your mirrors to become aware of the traffic situation on the new road.

Speed

Return to normal traffic speed by accelerating smoothly to blend with the traffic around you. In light traffic, accelerate moderately. In heavier traffic, you may have to accelerate more quickly. In a vehicle with manual transmission, shift gears as you increase speed.

II. Stop intersection

The approach

This driving task is done at intersections where you must come to a stop. It begins at the point where you can see the intersection and ends just before you enter the intersection. Be sure to follow these actions:

Traffic check

Before slowing down, look all around you. Use your mirrors to check traffic behind you.

Speed

Steadily reduce speed as you approach the intersection. In a vehicle with manual transmission, you may downshift into a lower gear as you slow down. Do not coast with your foot on the clutch pedal.

Space

While slowing down, keep at least a two to three-second distance behind the vehicle in front of you.

The stop

This driving task includes the actions you take while stopped and waiting to move through the intersection. Remember these points:

Stop

Come to a complete stop. Do not let your vehicle roll forward or backward. When traffic conditions allow, move forward to check that the way is clear or start across the intersection. If you have to stop after you have passed the stop line, do not back up.

Space

When stopped behind another vehicle at the intersection, leave enough space to pull out and pass without having to back up. Leaving this space protects you in three ways: it lets you pull around the vehicle in front if it stalls; it helps prevent you from being pushed into the vehicle ahead if you are hit from behind; and it reduces the risk of collision if the vehicle ahead rolls backward or backs up.

Stop line

If you are the first vehicle approaching an intersection with a red light or stop sign, stop behind the stop line if it is marked on the pavement. If there is no stop line, stop at the crosswalk, marked or not. If there is no crosswalk, stop at the edge of the sidewalk. If there is no sidewalk, stop at the edge of the intersection.

Driving through

This task includes the actions you take as you drive through the intersection and return to normal traffic speed. Make sure to follow these actions:

Traffic check

If you are stopped, waiting for a green light or for the way to be clear, keep checking traffic all around you. Just before entering the intersection, look left, ahead and right to check that the way is clear. If there is any doubt about the right-of-way, try to make eye contact with nearby drivers or pedestrians. You have not properly checked traffic if another vehicle or pedestrian has the right-of-way and must take action to avoid your vehicle.

Both hands

Keep both hands on the steering wheel as you drive through the intersection. You are most at risk from other traffic when you are crossing the intersection. Using both hands on the wheel gives you maximum steering control when you need it most. An exception to this is if you have a disability that prevents you from using both hands.

Gears

In a vehicle with manual transmission, do not shift gears crossing the intersection. If you need to, you may shift gears immediately after the vehicle is moving but before it is well into the intersection. You may also shift gears in an intersection wider than four lanes if not doing so would slow down other traffic. Generally, not changing gears gives you more control over your vehicle.

Traffic check

As you return to normal traffic speed, check your mirrors to become aware of the traffic situation after you have gone through the intersection.

Speed

Move ahead within four to five seconds after it is safe to start. Return to normal traffic speed by accelerating smoothly to blend with the traffic around you. In light traffic, accelerate moderately. In heavier traffic, you may have to accelerate more quickly. In a vehicle with manual transmission, shift gears as you increase speed.

III. Through intersection

The approach

This driving task is done at intersections where you may not need to stop. It begins at the point where you can see the intersection and ends just before the entrance to the intersection. Remember to do the following:

Traffic check

As you approach the intersection, look left and right for traffic on the intersecting road. If you have to slow down for the intersection, check your mirrors for traffic behind you.

Speed

Keep at the same speed as you go through the intersection unless there is a chance traffic may cross the intersection in front of you. If so, slow down or hold your foot over the brake, ready to slow down or stop. Watch for pedestrians about to cross the intersection and vehicles edging into the intersection or approaching at higher speeds.

Space

Keep at least a two to three-second distance behind the vehicle in front of you.

Driving through

This driving task includes your actions from the time you enter the intersection until you have crossed it and are returning to normal traffic speed. Remember these points:

Lane

Do not go over lane markings or change lanes in the intersection. If your lane is blocked by a vehicle turning left or a vehicle edging into the intersection from the right, slow down or stop instead of pulling out to go around the vehicle.

Both hands

Keep both hands on the steering wheel as you drive through the intersection. You are most at risk from other traffic when you are crossing the intersection. Using both hands on the wheel gives you maximum steering control when you need it most. An exception to this is if you have a disability that prevents you from using both hands.

Gears

In a vehicle with manual transmission, do not shift gears while crossing the intersection. If you need to, you may shift gears immediately after the vehicle is moving but before it is well into the intersection. You may also shift gears in an intersection wider than four lanes if not doing so would slow down other traffic. Generally, not changing gears gives you more control over your vehicle.

Traffic check

If you slowed down for the intersection, check your mirrors again before returning to normal traffic speed.

IV. Freeway

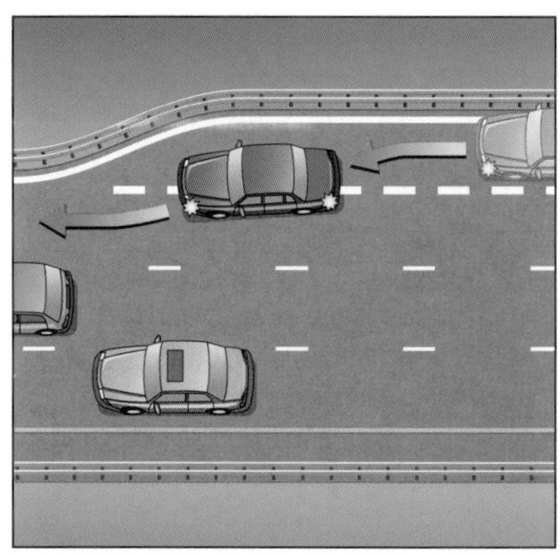

Entering

This driving task begins on the entrance ramp to a freeway and ends when you have reached the speed of the traffic on the freeway. Remember to do the following:

Traffic check

While on the ramp, as soon as you can see freeway traffic approaching from behind, check your mirrors and blind spot for a space to merge safely. At the same time, watch any vehicles in front of you on the ramp and keep back a safe distance. Continue to divide your attention between watching in front, checking your mirrors and looking over your shoulder to check your blind spot until you can merge safely with traffic.

Signal

If you have not done so already, turn on your signal as soon as traffic on the freeway is able to see your vehicle on the ramp.

Space

While on the ramp and merging with freeway traffic, keep at least a two to three-second distance behind the vehicle in front of you. Time your merge so you do not move in beside another vehicle or into the blind spot of another vehicle. If traffic is heavy or moving at such a high speed that it is difficult to keep an ideal following distance, adjust your speed to get the best spacing possible. While on the ramp and in the acceleration lane, keep inside the lane markings.

Speed

On the curve of the entrance ramp, keep your speed slow enough so that objects and people inside your vehicle are not pushed from the force created by turning the curve. While in the acceleration lane, increase your speed to match that of freeway traffic. While merging, control your speed to blend smoothly with freeway traffic.

Merge

Merge with freeway traffic in a smooth, gradual movement to the centre of the nearest freeway lane.

Cancel signal

Turn off your signal as soon as you have merged with freeway traffic.

Driving along

This driving task checks your actions driving along the freeway (but not merging, changing lanes or exiting). Be sure to remember the following points:

Traffic check

While driving along, keep checking traffic all around you and look in your mirrors every 5 to 10 seconds.

Speed

Avoid exceeding the speed limit or driving unreasonably slowly. Whenever possible, drive at a steady speed. Look ahead to where you are going to be in the next 12 to 15 seconds for dangerous situations or obstacles that you can avoid by changing your speed.

Space

Always keep at least a two to three-second distance behind the vehicle in front of you. If another vehicle follows too closely behind you, give yourself even more room in front or change lanes. Try to keep a space on both sides of your vehicle and try not to drive in the blind spots of other vehicles. Avoid driving behind large vehicles. Because of their size, they block your view of traffic more than other vehicles.

Exiting

This driving task begins when you are driving in the far right lane of the freeway and can see the exit you want to take. It ends when you reach the end of the exit ramp. Remember to do the following:

Traffic check

Before moving into the exit lane, look left and right and check your mirrors. If there is a lane of traffic on your right, such as an acceleration lane from an entrance ramp or a paved shoulder, remember also to check your right blind spot.

Signal

Turn on your signal before you reach the exit lane.

Exit lane

Enter the exit lane at the beginning of the lane with a smooth, gradual movement. Stay inside the lane markings. If there are two or more exit lanes, do not cross solid lines on the pavement to change lanes.

Speed

Do not slow down before you are completely in the exit lane. Once you are in the lane, slow gradually without causing traffic to pile up behind you. On the curve of the exit ramp, keep your speed slow enough so that objects and people inside your vehicle are not pushed from the force created by turning the curve. In a vehicle with manual transmission, downshift as you reduce speed.

Space

Keep at least a two to three-second distance behind the vehicle in front of you.

Cancel signal

Turn off your signal once you are on the exit ramp.

V. Lane change

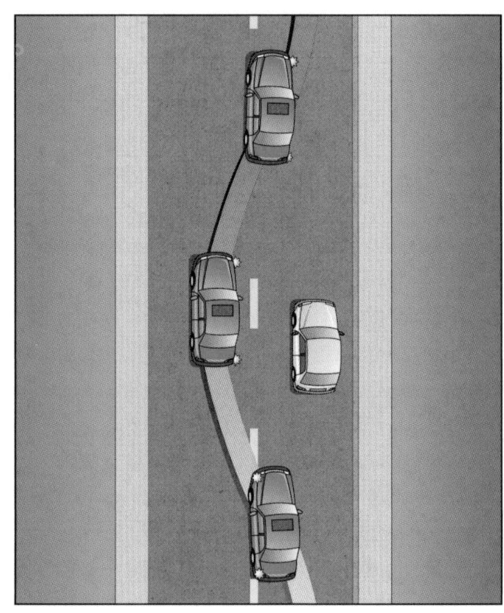

This driving task begins as you look for a space to change lanes and ends when you have completed the lane change. Remember to follow these actions:

Traffic check

While waiting to change lanes safely, look all around you. Divide your attention between watching in front, watching the mirrors and checking your blind spot. If there is another lane beside the one you are moving into, check traffic in that lane to avoid colliding with a vehicle moving into the lane at the same time as you do.

Signal

Turn on your signal when there is enough space for you to change lanes. After signalling, check your blind spot one more time before starting to move into the other lane. Your signal should be on soon enough to give traffic behind you time to react to the signal. If traffic in the lane you are moving into is heavy, you may turn on your signal before there is enough space to change lanes. This will let traffic behind you know that you are looking for a space to change lanes.

Space

Keep at least a two to three-second distance behind the vehicle in front of you. If there is another lane beside the one you are moving into, be careful not to move in beside another vehicle or into the blind spot of another vehicle.

Speed

Adjust your speed to match the speed of traffic in the new lane.

Change

Change lanes with a smooth, gradual movement into the centre of the new lane.

Both hands

Keep both hands on the steering wheel as you change lanes. Using both hands on the wheel gives you maximum steering control. An exception to this is if you have a disability that prevents you from using both hands.

Cancel signal

Turn off your signal as soon as you have changed lanes.

VI. Roadside stop

The approach

This driving task begins when the examiner tells you to stop and ends once you have come to a stop. Make sure you take these actions:

Traffic check

Before slowing down, check your mirrors and scan to see if it is legal (look for signs) to make the roadside stop. Then scan the road for traffic approaching from the front and rear of your vehicle. A 150 metre gap in both directions provides enough space to perform the move safely. If there is a chance of traffic or pedestrians overtaking you on the right, check your right blind spot just before pulling over.

Signal

Turn on your signal before slowing down unless there are vehicles waiting to enter the road from sideroads or driveways between you and the point where you intend to stop. Wait until you have passed these entrances so that drivers will not think you are turning before the stopping point.

Speed

Steadily reduce speed as you approach the stop. In a vehicle with manual transmission, you may downshift into a lower gear as you slow down. Do not coast with your foot on the clutch pedal.

Position

Stop parallel to the curb and not more than about 30 centimetres away from it. If there is no curb, stop as far as possible off the travelled part of the road. Do not stop where you will block an entrance or other traffic.

The stop

This driving task includes the actions you take after stopping. Remember to do the following:

Signal

Turn off your signal and turn on your hazard lights.

Park

If your vehicle has an automatic transmission, put the gear selector in park and set the parking brake. If your vehicle has a manual transmission, set the parking brake and shift into neutral if not turning off the engine, or shift into low or reverse if turning off the engine. When parking on a hill, turn your wheels in the appropriate direction to keep your vehicle from rolling.

Resume

This driving task begins when the examiner tells you to move back onto the road and ends when you have returned to normal traffic speed. Take the following actions:

Start

Turn on the engine. Release the parking brake and select the correct gear to move back onto the road.

Signal
Turn off your hazard lights and turn on your left turn signal.

Traffic check
Just before pulling away from the stop, check your mirrors and your left blind spot.

Speed
Return to normal traffic speed by accelerating smoothly to blend with the traffic around you. In light traffic, accelerate moderately. In heavier traffic, you may have to accelerate more quickly. In a vehicle with manual transmission, shift gears as you increase speed.

Cancel signal
Turn off your signal as soon as you are back on the road.

VII. Curve

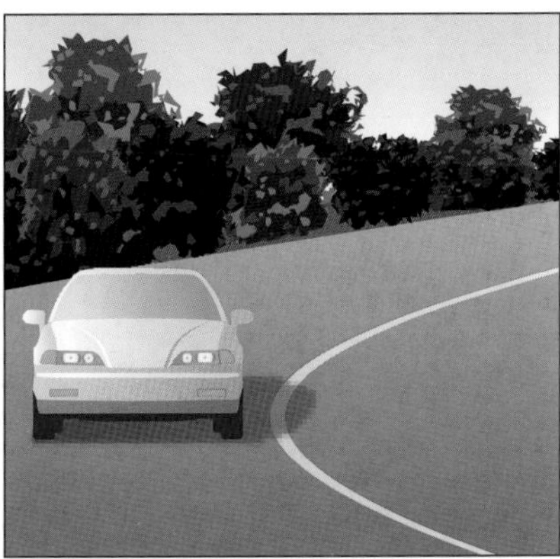

This driving task begins when the curve comes into sight and ends when you have gone completely around it. Follow these actions:

Speed
As you approach the curve, try to determine the safe speed for the curve. To do this, look for clues such as a sign that shows the safe speed, the shape of the curve and the type of road you are driving on. Slow down to the safe speed for the curve by the time you are 30 metres into it. In a blind curve where you cannot see all the way around it, drive more slowly in case oncoming traffic wanders into your lane or the curve is tighter than you expected. **Slow down before the start of the curve to avoid braking in the curve.** While in the curve, keep your speed steady and slow enough so that objects and people inside your vehicle are not pushed from the force created by turning on the curve. Near the end of the curve, begin accelerating to return to normal speed. In a vehicle with manual transmission,

do not shift gears in the curve. Not changing gears gives you more control over your vehicle and reduces the risk of your wheels locking while downshifting.

Lane

As you enter the curve, look across or as far around it as possible. This helps you stay in a smooth line and centred in the lane throughout the curve. If you look only at the road directly in front of you, you are likely to wander back and forth across the lane, forcing you to constantly correct your steering.

VIII. Business section

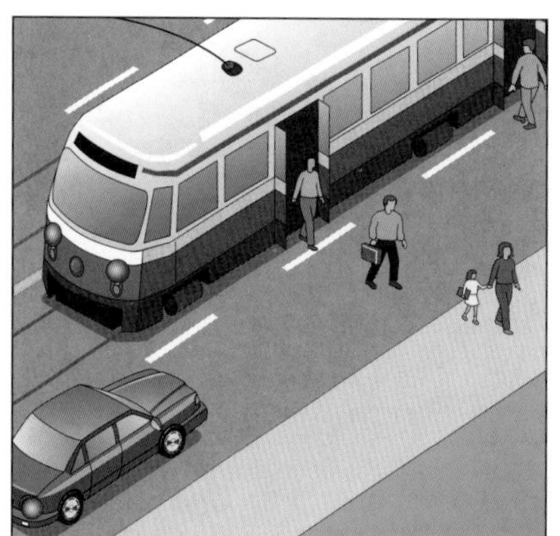

This driving task is done on straight sections of road where a number of businesses are located. Be sure to do the following actions:

Traffic check

In a business area, there are many places other than intersections where vehicles or pedestrians are likely to enter the road. These include entrances to businesses, institutions and construction sites, as well as pedestrian and railway crossings. At all these locations, look left and right to check for vehicles or pedestrians about to enter the road.

Mirror check

While driving along, check your mirrors every 5 to 10 seconds. Check your mirrors more often in heavy traffic or where vehicles are moving at different speeds.

Lane

Drive in the safest lane for through traffic. This is usually the curb lane. However, if the curb lane is blocked by traffic or there are many curbside hazards, the centre lane may be a safer choice. Keep to the centre of the lane and within the lane markings. Look ahead to where you will be in the next 12 to 15 seconds for dangerous situations or obstacles that you can avoid by changing lanes.

IX. Residential section

Speed

Avoid exceeding the speed limit or driving unreasonably slowly. Whenever possible, drive at a steady speed. Look ahead to where you will be in the next 12 to 15 seconds for dangerous situations or obstacles that you can avoid by changing your speed.

Space

Keep at least a two to three-second distance behind the vehicle in front of you. Increase the distance if another vehicle follows too closely behind you. On a multi-lane road, try to keep a space on both sides of your vehicle and try not to drive in the blind spots of other vehicles. In slow traffic, avoid driving behind large vehicles that block your view of traffic ahead of you. When you stop behind another vehicle, leave enough space to see its rear wheels or to pull around it without having to back up.

This driving task is done on straight sections of residential or rural road. Remember these points:

Traffic check

On a residential road, watch out for entrances to schools, pedestrian crossings, driveways, sidewalks and any other locations where there might be traffic hazards. On a rural road, watch for entrances to residences, farms, businesses and industrial sites. At all these locations, look left and right to check for vehicles or pedestrians about to enter the road.

Mirror check

While driving along, check your mirrors every 5 to 10 seconds. Check your mirrors more often in heavy traffic or where vehicles are moving at different speeds.

Lane

Keep to the centre of the lane. If there are no lane markings, keep to the centre of the travelled part of the road, away from parked vehicles or pedestrians. Where you cannot see far ahead on the road because of a curve or a hill, move right to avoid colliding with an oncoming vehicle that is over the centre line. Look ahead to where you will be in the next 12 to 15 seconds for dangerous situations or obstacles that you can avoid by changing lanes.

Speed

Avoid exceeding the speed limit or driving unreasonably slowly. Whenever possible, drive at a steady speed. Look ahead to where you will be in the next 12 to 15 seconds for dangerous situations or obstacles that you can avoid by changing your speed.

Space

Keep at least a two to three-second distance behind the vehicle in front of you. Increase the distance if another vehicle follows too closely behind you. In slow traffic, avoid driving behind large vehicles that block your view of traffic ahead. When you stop behind another vehicle, leave enough space to see its rear wheels or to pull around it without having to back up.

X. Parallel park

The approach

This driving task begins when the examiner tells you to park and ends when you have come to a stop, ready to back into the parking space. Remember these points:

Traffic check

Before slowing down, check your mirror for traffic behind you. Before pulling into position to back up, check your blind spot.

Signal

Turn on your signal before slowing down unless there are vehicles waiting to enter the road from sideroads or driveways between you and your stopping point. Wait until you have passed these entrances so that drivers will not think you are turning before your parallel parking position.

Speed

Steadily reduce speed. In a vehicle with manual transmission, you may downshift into a lower gear as you slow down. Do not coast with your foot on the clutch pedal.

Stop

Stop beside, or parallel to, the parked vehicle (real or imaginary) in front of the empty parking space. Leave at least 60 centimetres between your vehicle and the parked vehicle. Stop when your vehicle is completely in front of the empty parking space.

Park

This driving task includes the actions you take to park in a parallel parking space. Remember to do the following:

Traffic check

Before backing up, look all around the vehicle and check your mirrors and both blind spots. Do not start reversing until the way is clear or traffic has stopped to let you park.

Back up

Begin reversing into the space, turning the steering wheel towards the curb. When your vehicle is about halfway into the space, steer to bring your vehicle in line with the curb. Once you are in the parking space, move forward or backward to fit within the pavement markings or to allow room for the vehicle in front or behind you to pull out. Do not hit the curb or touch another vehicle while entering your parking space. Where there is no curb, park off the travelled part of the road.

Park

If your vehicle has an automatic transmission, put the gear selector in park and set the parking brake. If your vehicle has a manual transmission, set the parking brake and shift into neutral if not turning off the engine, or shift into low or reverse if turning off the engine. When parking on a hill, turn your wheels in the appropriate direction to keep your vehicle from rolling.

Resume

This driving task begins when the examiner tells you to move from the parking space and ends when you have returned to normal traffic speed. Remember these points:

Start

Turn on the engine. Release the parking brake and select the correct gear to move back onto the road.

Signal

Turn on your signal.

Traffic check

Just before pulling out of the parking spot, check your mirrors and your blind spot.

Speed

Return to normal traffic speed by accelerating smoothly to blend with the traffic around you. In light traffic, accelerate moderately. In heavier traffic, you may have to accelerate more quickly. In a vehicle with manual transmission, shift gears as you increase speed.

Cancel signal

Turn off your signal after you leave the parking space.

XI. Three-point turn

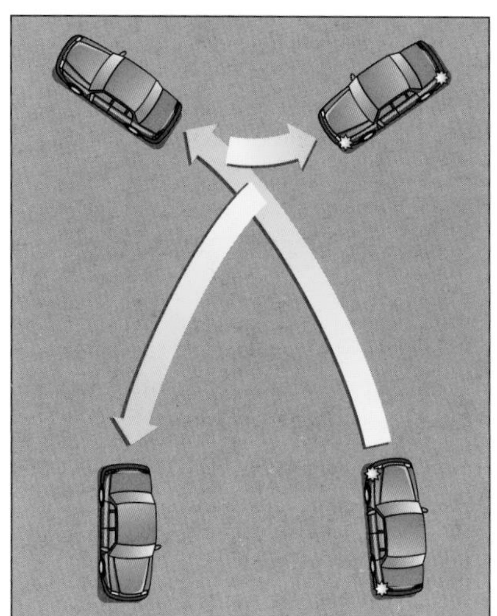

The approach

This driving task begins when the examiner tells you to stop and turn your vehicle around. It ends when you have almost stopped, ready to start the turn. Be sure to do the following:

Traffic check

Before slowing down, check traffic in front and behind you. If necessary, check your blind spot before pulling over to the right side of the road to stop.

Signal

Turn on your signal before slowing down unless there are vehicles waiting to enter the road from sideroads or driveways between you and your stopping point. Wait until you have passed these entrances so that drivers will not think you are turning.

Speed

Steadily reduce speed. In a vehicle with manual transmission, you may downshift into a lower gear as you slow down. Do not coast with your foot on the clutch pedal.

Position

Stop so you are parallel to the curb and not more than 30 centimetres away. Where there is no curb, stop as far as possible off the travelled part of the road. Do not stop where you will block an entrance or other traffic.

Turn around

This driving task includes the actions you take to turn around and ends when you are ready to drive away in the opposite direction. Remember these points:

Traffic check

Check your mirrors and your blind spot just before starting the turn. Wait until the way is clear or traffic has stopped to let you turn. Each time you stop while turning, check traffic in both directions.

Signal

Turn on your left signal before starting to turn.

Turn around

With the steering wheel turned sharply left, move slowly and smoothly across the road. When you have reached the far left side of the road, stop and put your vehicle in reverse. With the steering wheel turned sharply right, reverse so the vehicle is facing in the new direction. Stop and shift into forward gear to move ahead. Use the whole road to make your turn, reversing only once. Do not reverse over the edge or shoulder of the road or into the curb.

Resume

This driving task begins when you are turned around, ready to move ahead and ends when you have returned to normal traffic speed. Make sure you take these actions:

Traffic check

Check your mirrors before increasing speed.

Speed

Return to normal traffic speed by accelerating smoothly to blend with the traffic around you. In light traffic, accelerate moderately. In heavier traffic, you may have to accelerate more quickly. In a vehicle with manual transmission, shift gears as you increase speed.

Part Two

Off-Road Vehicles

Introduction

Off-road vehicles and snowmobiles are popular forms of recreation for many people in Ontario. They are also necessary for transportation in remote areas and in emergencies. But these vehicles are not toys. If you intend to use them, you must know how they work, how to drive them safely in different situations and how Ontario laws apply to them.

It is important to remember that off-road vehicles are intended for off-road use. Dirt bikes cannot be driven on public roads, although snowmobiles can be in some areas. Off-road vehicles are allowed to travel directly across some highways. However only single-rider all-terrain vehicles can be driven on the shoulder of some provincial highways and municipal roads where by-laws permit. vehicles can be driven on the shoulder of some provincial highways and municipal roads where by-laws permit.

This section of the handbook contains information about Ontario's laws and safe driving tips for snowmobiles and off-road vehicles. As you read, remember it is a guide only. For official purposes, please refer to the Highway Traffic Act, the Motorized Snow Vehicles Act, the Off-Road Vehicles Act, the Trespass to Property Act and the Occupiers' Liability Act of Ontario. The applicable legislation can be accessed online through Ontario's e-Laws website (www.e-laws.gov.on.ca).

Note: Alcohol presents a major risk to your safety and the safety of others whether you are driving a car, motorcycle, snowmobile or off-road vehicle. Drinking affects your ability to operate your vehicle and increases your chances of having a collision.

CONTENTS — Part Two

Chapter 1

DRIVING A SNOWMOBILE

This chapter tells you what you need to know to drive a motorized snow vehicle in Ontario. This includes age requirements, registration, where you can and cannot drive, safety tips, traffic signs and signals and the Snowmobiler's Code of Ethics.

I. Getting ready to drive a snowmobile

What you need to drive a snowmobile in Ontario

You can drive a snowmobile if you have a valid Ontario driver's licence (any class). If you do not have a driver's licence and you are 12 years of age or older, a valid motorized snow vehicle operator's licence will allow you to drive on trails established and maintained by a recreational organization for the use of snowmobiles. However, you must be 16 years of age or older and have a driver's licence or a motorized snow vehicle operator's licence (not both) to drive a snowmobile along or across a public road where snowmobiles are allowed.

A motorized snow vehicle operator's licence is issued by the Ontario Federation of Snowmobile Clubs in co-operation with the Ministry of Transportation. You must successfully pass a snowmobile driver training course to get a licence. (For more information on how to get a motorized snow vehicle operator's licence, see the section Take A Snowmobile Driver Training Course on page 193).

If you are a visitor to Ontario and wish to drive a snowmobile while you are here, you must have a valid licence that allows you to drive a snowmobile in your home province, state or country.

You must carry your driver's licence or snow vehicle operator's licence when you are driving your snowmobile anywhere other than on your own property. You must show it when asked by a police

or conservation officer.

If your driver's licence or snow vehicle operator's licence has been suspended, you may not drive any type of vehicle on or off any roads or in any public place.

Registering and insuring your snowmobile

Before driving a snowmobile, it must be registered with the Ministry of Transportation through a Driver and Vehicle Licence Issuing Office. This applies to new, used snowmobiles that have never been registered, and snowmobiles previously registered in another jurisdiction. If you buy a new snowmobile it must be registered within six days of sale.

If you buy a new snowmobile your dealer will register it with the Ministry of Transportation within six days of the sale. If you buy a used snowmobile that has been previously registered, you will simply need the signed snow vehicle permit and the bill of sale to transfer the registration into your name.

You must pay a fee to register your snowmobile. This is a one-time fee to be paid by the owner of the snowmobile. After registering, you will be given a permit and a registration number decal to display on your snowmobile.

Attach the decal to each side of your snowmobile's cowling or engine cover. It should be placed so that the start of the registration number is between 10 and 15 centimetres from the rear of the cowling. If the decal cannot be placed on the cowling because of the design of the vehicle, place the decal on each side of the tunnel, near the light reflector.

Unless you are driving your registered snowmobile on your own property or you are a resident of Northern Ontario that is exempt, you must have a validation sticker on your registration decal. You must carry your driver's licence or MSVOL and evidence of your vehicle's registration at all times and show it to a police or conservation officer when asked.

Snowmobiles are only permitted on public highways when directly crossing. In specific circumstances, snowmobiles can operate on the non-serviced portion of some highways. Local municipalities also have authority to pass by-laws governing the use of snowmobiles on highways under their authority.

There is an annual renewal fee for the sticker. Place the sticker in the upper right corner of the decal.

You must also have liability insurance to drive your snowmobile off your own property. Carry the insurance card given to you by the insurance company for the snowmobile and show it when a police or conservation officer asks for it. If someone else uses your snowmobile with your consent, you are both responsible for any penalties, damages or injuries that may occur.

There are separate requirements and rules regarding the operation of trail grooming equipment. Make sure you know what is required before operating grooming equipment.

Wear a helmet

You must wear a helmet whenever you drive or ride on a snowmobile or on any kind of toboggan or sled towed by a snowmobile. Although you do not require a helmet when you operate a snowmobile on your own land, it is recommended that you wear one for safety reasons. The helmet must meet the standards approved for motorcycle helmets, or motor assisted bicycle helmets, and must be fastened properly under the chin.

Protect your eyes and face

Always wear a face shield or goggles. A face shield can help prevent windburn, frostbite, sunblindness and watering eyes from the wind. A face shield can also protect your eyes from branches and twigs when driving through wooded areas. Select lightly tinted and shatterproof shields or goggles to match conditions. For example, choose clear plastic for dull, cloudy days and deep yellow for late afternoon when flat light can hide depressions in the snow. Avoid dark tinted shields or goggles, which can restrict your vision.

Make sure your snowmobile is in good condition

Before every trip, check your snowmobile to make sure it is in good working order. Your life may depend upon it. Do the following:

- Check the steering mechanism. Turn the handlebars back and forth to make sure the turning is smooth and unrestricted.
- Check the condition and tension of the motor drive belt. Change it if necessary or if you are in doubt about its reliability.
- Check the emergency switch, headlights and tail lights.
- Check the battery solution level.
- Check the throttle and brake levers. Make sure they move freely.
- Check the spark plugs and the tank's fuel level. Do not use matches or a lighter when doing this and never add fuel when the motor is running.

When towing a toboggan, sled or any other kind of vehicle behind a snowmobile, be sure to use a rigid tow-bar

When towing, use a rigid tow-bar and safety chain.

and a safety chain. For safety, towed vehicles must have reflective material on the front sides, rear sides and rear to make them more visible. Towing is generally not allowed on public roads except to cross the road at a 90-degree angle. This does not apply to a snowmobile being used to free a stuck vehicle, for any emergency rescue or for trail maintenance.

Before you drive anywhere, read the owner's manual carefully and keep it in your snowmobile at all times.

Be well prepared for every trip

Carefully preparing for every trip is an important part of safe snowmobiling. Check local weather forecasts and local ice conditions before heading out as they can change in a matter of hours. Avoid traveling on unmarked frozen lakes and rivers. Make sure you tell someone where you will be traveling and when you expect to be back. Use the buddy system; do not drive your snowmobile alone and always ride within your abilities and according to conditions.

Take along a first aid kit, a vehicle repair kit, an extra ignition key, a drive belt, spark plugs and a rope. On long trips, include a map and a compass (or a GPS unit and know how to use it), flashlight, hunting knife, hatchet, extra fuel, matches in a waterproof box and high energy food such as granola bars. If you travel over frozen lakes and rivers, wear a buoyant snowmobile suit and carry ice picks to improve the chances of survival if you break through the ice.

II. Safe and responsible snowmobiling

Where you can and cannot drive

You may drive your registered snowmobile on your own property, on the private trails of organizations to which you belong, on private property when you have the owner's permission or in permitted public parks and conservation areas.

Snowmobiles are only permitted on public highways when directly crossing. In specific circumstances, snowmobiles can operate on the non-serviced portion of some highways. Local municipalities also have the authority to pass by-laws governing the use of snowmobiles on highways

under their authority.

You may not drive a snowmobile on certain high-speed roads, freeways, the Queen Elizabeth Way, the Ottawa Queensway and the Kitchener-Waterloo Expressway. This includes the area around these roads, from fence line to fence line. You may not drive on the serviced section of a road (from shoulder to shoulder) except to cross. When crossing, you must slow down, stop and then proceed at a 90 degree angle. When riding in a group, do not motion the driver behind you to cross. Let each rider assess oncoming traffic and decide for themselves when it is safe to cross. If visibility is restricted at the crossing, you may then wave to the driver behind you that the way is clear.

Except where prohibited, you may drive your snowmobile along public roads, keeping as far away from the road as possible in the section between the shoulder and the fence line. Local municipalities may pass by-laws that regulate or prohibit snowmobiles anywhere within their boundaries, on or off public roads. Make sure you are aware of the by-laws in the municipality where you intend to snowmobile.

You may not drive a snowmobile on railway tracks unless you have permission from the railway track authority.

Public trails

Ontario's public trails are established and maintained by many snowmobile clubs. They are patrolled by Ontario Provincial Police, municipal police, conservation officers and Snowmobile Trail Officer Patrol (STOP) officers. Some clubs require snowmobiles to have and display a trail permit to drive on their trails. Some other clubs allow their trails to be used without a trail permit. Trails may have signs stating that a trail permit is required. If you are unsure, check with the local snowmobile club to find out if you need a trail permit.

For trails operated by the Ontario Federation of Snowmobile Clubs, you must have and display a trail permit. This includes trails on private property, municipal property and land owned by the government. Some snowmobile trail user groups are exempt from the trail permit requirement. Those who are eligible for exemption and the documents required as proof are included in the

Watch for trail and highway signs.

trail permits section of the regulations of the Motorized Snow Vehicles Act. Snowmobilers who are exempt must carry the appropriate documents and show them when requested to do so.

For information about trails and trail permits, contact your local snowmobile club or the Ontario Federation of Snowmobile Clubs, 501 Welham Road, Unit 9, Barrie, ON L4N 8Z6. Phone 705-739-7669; fax 705-739-5005; or e-mail at info@ofsc.on.ca. You can visit the OFSC website at www.ofsc.on.ca

Do not trespass

You are trespassing if you drive your snowmobile on private property without permission from the owner. The owner is not required to have a "No Trespassing" sign posted. If you are driving your snowmobile on private property, you must stop and identify yourself when asked by the police, the owner of the property or a representative of the owner. If you are told to leave the property, you must do so immediately.

You may be fined up to $2,000 if you are convicted of trespassing. In addition, you may be ordered to pay damages up to $1,000. Under certain circumstances, you may also be required to pay for the cost of prosecuting. Charges will be laid against the driver of the snowmobile. If the driver is not known, the owner may be charged if the snowmobile was used with the owner's permission.

A copy of the Trespass to Property Act is available through Publications Ontario. Phone (416) 326-5300 or 1-800-668-9938. It is available over the Internet at www.publications.gov.on.ca and www.e-laws.gov.on.ca.

It is an offence under the Railway Safety Act to trespass on railway tracks.

Obey the speed limits

You must not drive a snowmobile faster than 20 km/h in any public park or exhibition ground or on any road where the speed limit for other vehicles is 50 km/h or less. You must not drive faster than 50 km/h on snowmobile trails or on any road where the speed limit for other vehicles is more than 50 km/h. Always leave extra space between you and the snowmobile in front to give yourself more time to react to unexpected hazards and to stop safely. Lower your speed at night and don't outrun your headlights. Reduced night time visibility makes hazards more difficult to spot and estimating distance is much harder. Always wear clothing with reflective markings to remain visible at night.

Municipalities may set other speed limits for snowmobiles on public roads, trails and parks within their boundaries. Check municipal by-laws.

Stop for police

You must come to a safe stop when requested by a police officer to do so. If you do not stop, you may have to pay a fine, or go to jail, or both. If you are convicted of failing to stop for a police officer and the court believes you wilfully avoided police during pursuit — that you tried to escape the police — your licence will be suspended for a minimum of five years. Your licence can be suspended for up to ten years if anyone is killed or injured as a result of avoiding police.

Report collisions to the police

You must report to the police immediately any collision that results in injury to any person or damage to property apparently exceeding $400.

Do not drink and drive

Alcohol is a major factor in snowmobile fatalities. Consuming any amount of alcohol before you ride affects your ability to make good decisions. Alcohol also increases fatigue, slows reaction time and increases your risk of hypothermia.

It is against the law to drive a snowmobile when you are impaired by alcohol or drugs.

Drinking and driving is a deadly combination. All drivers, especially inexperienced drivers, must be able to concentrate on driving.

Consuming any amount of alcohol before you ride affects your ability to make good decisions. Even one drink can reduce your ability to concentrate and react to things that happen suddenly when you are driving. With more alcohol in your blood, you could have trouble judging distances and your vision may become blurred. Factors like tiredness, your mood, and how long ago you ate and how much, can make a difference in how alcohol affects your driving ability.

The police can stop any driver to determine if alcohol or drug testing is required. They may also do roadside spot checks. When stopped by the police, you may be told to blow into a machine that tests your breath for alcohol, a roadside screening device, or perform physical co-ordination tests. If you fail or refuse to provide a breath sample or to perform the physical co-ordination tests, you will be charged under the *Criminal Code*.

If the reading on the machine shows you have been drinking, you may be taken to a police station for a breathalyzer test. The breathalyzer uses your breath to measure the amount of alcohol in your bloodstream.

If you cannot give a breath sample or it is impracticable to obtain a sample of breath, the police officer can require you to provide a blood sample instead.

If the police believe that a driver is impaired because of the consumption of a drug or a combination of alcohol and a drug, the police can also require a driver to submit to an evaluation and then require a driver to provide blood, oral fluid or urine samples. If you fail or refuse to comply with any of these demands, you will be charged under the *Criminal Code*.

Driving impaired or with more than 80 milligrams of alcohol in 100 millilitres of blood (.08) is an offence under the *Criminal Code*. Even if your blood alcohol concentration is less than .08, you can still be charged with impaired driving under the *Criminal Code*.

You will receive an immediate 90-day Administrative Driver's Licence Suspension if your blood alcohol concentration (BAC) is more than .08 or if you fail or refuse to provide a breath or bodily fluid sample, perform a physical co-ordination test or submit to an evaluation.

If you register in the "warn range" of .05 to .08 on a roadside screening device, you will receive an **immediate** driver's licence suspension. For a first occurrence, you will be suspended for 3 days. For a second occurrence in a five-year period, you will be immediately suspended for 7 days and you must undergo a remedial alcohol education program. For a third or subsequent time in a five-year period, you will be immediately suspended for 30 days and you must undergo a remedial alcohol treatment program and have an ignition interlock condition placed on your licence for 6 months. If you choose not to install an ignition interlock device, you must not drive until the condition is removed from your licence.

If you are 21 years old and under and hold a full class driver's licence you must not drive if you have been drinking alcohol. Your blood alcohol level must be zero. If you are caught driving with alcohol in your blood, you will receive an immediate driver's licence suspension at the roadside for 24 hours and, if convicted, you will face a fine of $60-$500 and a 30-day licence suspension.

Drivers of all ages in either Level One or Level Two of Ontario's graduated licensing system must also have a blood alcohol level of zero when driving. New drivers caught drinking and driving will receive an immediate driver's licence suspension at the roadside for 24 hours and, if convicted, will face a fine of $60–$500 and will receive a suspension period as per the Novice Driver Escalating Sanctions scheme. For the first occurrence, you will be suspended for 30 days. For the second occurrence, in a five-year period, you will be suspended for 90 days. For the third occurrence in a five-year period, the novice portion of your driver's licence will be cancelled and you must reapply for a G1 licence.

Novice drivers will also be charged under the *Criminal Code* if their BAC exceeds .08 and will be issued a warn range suspension if they register between .05 and .08.

Drugs

Any drug that changes your mood or the way you see and feel about the world around you will affect the way you drive. *Criminal Code* and HTA sanctions apply to drivers impaired by alcohol or a drug.

In circumstances involving possible impairment by drugs or a combination of alcohol and a drug, police can require a driver to perform physical co-ordination tests and to submit to an evaluation and then require a driver to provide blood, oral fluid or urine samples. If you fail or refuse to comply with any of these demands, you will be charged under the *Criminal Code*. You will also receive an immediate 90-day Administrative Driver's Licence Suspension. Illegal drugs such as marijuana and cocaine are not the only problem. Some drugs that your doctor may prescribe for you and some over-the-counter drugs can also impair your driving.

Here are some points you should remember:

- If you use prescription medicines or get allergy shots, ask your doctor about side effects such as dizziness, blurred vision, nausea or drowsiness that could affect your driving.
- Read the information on the package of any over-the-counter medicine you take. Any stimulant, diet pill, tranquillizer or sedative may affect your driving. Even allergy and cold remedies may have ingredients that could affect your driving.
- Drugs and any amount of alcohol together can have dangerous effects, even several days after you have taken the drug. Do not take a chance — ask your doctor or pharmacist.

Practice safe snowmobiling

Driving a snowmobile requires the same attention and alertness that driving any other kind of vehicle does. You must have complete control of your reflexes. If you are a beginner, practice until you can handle the basic driving skills.

Learn how to control your balance on turns by using your weight to control your movements and leaning in the direction you want to turn. Position your body on the snowmobile in a way that will give you the most comfort and control for the conditions in which you are driving. On level ground, sit or kneel with both knees on the seat. On uneven or bumpy ground, stand on the running boards with your knees slightly bent.

Always take the time to plan your route before you ride and make sure others in your group know the route as well. If you must stop on the trail, always select a location where you will be visible and pull over to the right as far as possible. If you are riding in a group, you should park the snowmobiles in single file and leave the vehicles running so you are visible at night.

On hard-packed snow or ice, reduce your speed because stops and turns are harder to make and you will require greater distance to complete them. When your snowmobile is trapped in deep snow, remember to turn off the motor before you try to get it out of the snow.

Every time you travel on ice, you are risking your safety and that of your passenger. Watch out for pressure cracks which are much more difficult to spot at night. If you are in an unfamiliar area, ask local authorities or residents about the ice conditions, inlets, outlets, springs, fast-moving current or other hazards. Listen to local radio broadcast warnings by the Ontario Provincial Police about ice conditions. If you must drive over frozen lakes or rivers, you should consider using a buoyant snowmobile suit. It might save your life.

Whenever you are driving, always watch for trails and highway signs and obey them. Always remain on the right-hand side of the trail when riding and exercise caution on hills and curves. You should always be prepared for the unexpected. Exercise caution at road and rail crossings. Trucks and trains often kick up large clouds of snow that greatly reduce visibility. Carry a cell phone with you when riding.

III. Snowmobile signals and signs

Hand signals

Signals tell others what you want to do, giving them a chance to slow down, stop or prepare to turn. Use hand signals to signal before stopping, slowing down suddenly or turning. Give the correct signal well before the action and make sure others can see it. These illustrations show nationally recognized hand and arm signals.

Left turn

Extend your left arm straight out and point in the direction of the turn.

Right turn

Raise your left arm to shoulder height with elbow bent.

Stop

Extend your right arm straight up over your head with the palm of the hand flat.

Slowing

Extend your left arm out and down the side of your body. Flap your arm up and down to signal caution.

Oncoming snowmobiles

Raise your left arm to shoulder height with your elbow bent and motion left to right over your head, pointing to the right side of the trail.

Snowmobiles following

Raise left arm to shoulder height with your elbow bent. Motion front to back over your shoulder with your thumb, like a hitchhiker.

Last snowmobile in line

With elbow bent, raise your left forearm to shoulder height and clench your fist.

Trail signs

Trail signs give you important information about what to do in certain situations. Here are some common trail signs and what they mean. Because trail signs are not official traffic signs, they may vary in shape and colour. Watch for signs such as these and obey them.

Stop

A stop sign is eight-sided and has a red background with white letters. Come to a complete stop.

Stop ahead

Be prepared to stop for a stop sign up ahead.

Snowmobiling permitted

A sign with a green circle means you may do the activity shown inside the ring. You may drive a snowmobile in the area where this sign is displayed.

Snowmobiling restricted

A sign with a red circle with a line through it means the activity shown inside the ring is not allowed. Do not drive a snowmobile in the area where this sign is displayed.

Direction signs

These signs give you information about the direction in which you should travel on the trail. Do as the sign tells you.

Traffic signs

If you are driving your snowmobile along or across any public roads, you need to be aware of traffic signs and what they mean. The following traffic signs relate specifically to snowmobiles.

Snowmobiles permitted
Snowmobiles are allowed on the road or highway where this sign is displayed.

Snowmobiles restricted
Snowmobiles are not allowed on the road or highway where this sign is displayed.

Snowmobiles crossing
These signs warns drivers that snowmobiles are allowed to cross the road.

Wind chill factor

It is important to consider wind chill factor when planning outdoor winter activities.

Wind chill factor is the combined effect of wind and low temperature which makes it feel much colder on a windy day in winter than is the actual temperature. This is caused by the faster cooling effect of the wind. For example, if the actual temperature is -10°C and the wind speed is 40 km/h the temperature feels like -31°C.

You need to be aware of the wind chill factor so that you can dress appropriately. Outer layers that are waterproof and multiple under layers of clothing provide added protection, and allow you to take clothing off if temperatures increase. Also, make sure that young passengers are properly dressed and that their hands and faces are well protected. Wearing a balaclava will reduce the risk of exposure. Prolonged exposure to cold wind chill temperatures can lead to hypothermia.

The chart on the next page can help you calculate wind chill so you will be aware of potentially dangerous conditions.

Wind chill calculation chart

Observed wind speed at 10m elevation, in km/h	Air Temperature in °C 5	0	-5	-10	-15	-20	-25	-30	-35	-40	-45	-50
5	4	-2	-7	-13	-19	-24	-30	-36	-41	-47	-53	-58
10	3	-3	-9	-15	-21	-27	-33	-39	-45	-51	-57	-63
15	2	-4	-11	-17	-23	-29	-35	-41	-48	-54	-60	-66
20	1	-5	-12	-18	-24	-31	-37	-43	-49	-56	-62	-68
25	1	-6	-12	-19	-25	-32	-38	-45	-51	-57	-64	-70
30	0	-7	-13	-20	-26	-33	-39	-46	-52	-59	-65	-72
35	0	-7	-14	-20	-27	-33	-40	-47	-53	-60	-66	-73
40	-1	-7	-14	-21	-27	-34	-41	-48	-54	-61	-68	-74
45	-1	-8	-15	-21	-28	-35	-42	-48	-55	-62	-69	-75
50	-1	-8	-15	-22	-29	-35	-42	-49	-56	-63	-70	-76
55	-2	-9	-15	-22	-29	-36	-43	-50	-57	-63	-70	-77
60	-2	-9	-16	-23	-30	-37	-43	-50	-57	-64	-71	-78
65	-2	-9	-16	-23	-30	-37	-44	-51	-58	-65	-72	-79
70	-2	-9	-16	-23	-30	-37	-44	-51	-59	-66	-73	-80
75	-3	-10	-17	-24	-31	-38	-45	-52	-59	-66	-73	-80
80	-3	-10	-17	-24	-31	-38	-45	-52	-60	-67	-74	-81

Approximate Thresholds:

Wind Chill at or below -25°C: risk of frostbite in prolonged exposure.

Wind Chill at or below -35°C: frostbite possible in 10 minutes; warm skin, suddenly exposed. (Shorter time if skin is cool at the start.)

Wind Chill at or below -60°C: frostbite possible in less than 2 minutes; warm skin, suddenly exposed. (Shorter time if skin is cool at the start.)

Take a snowmobile driver training course

If you are between 12 and 15 years of age, or if you are 16 and older and do not have a valid Ontario driver's licence, you must successfully pass a snowmobile driver training course to get your operator's licence to drive a snowmobile. A snowmobile driver training course can also be a valuable refresher for licensed and experienced snowmobilers.

The course takes about six hours and is usually held over three days. It covers safe driving practices, snowmobile laws, knowledge of the snowmobile, maintenance, driving positions, survival, first aid, night driving, trail signs, clothing and storage. It also teaches safe and courteous driving habits and skills to help you avoid collisions and property damage.

The training course is offered by the Ontario Federation of Snowmobile Clubs (OFSC) in co-operation with the Ministry of Transportation and is offered by club instructors trained by the OFSC. For the location of the nearest OFSC member club offering the course and the cost, contact the OFSC Driver Training Office at 501 Welham Road, Unit 9, Barrie, ON, L4N 8Z6. Phone 705-739-7669 or fax 705-739-5005. You can visit the OFSC website at www.ofsc.on.ca.

The snowmobiler's code of ethics

Follow this code of ethics and you will do your part to make snowmobiling a respectable, fun and safe winter recreation.

1. I will be a good sportsperson and conservationist. I recognize that people judge all snowmobilers by my actions. I will use my influence with other snowmobilers to promote responsible conduct.
2. I will not litter trails or camping areas. I will not pollute lakes or streams. I will carry out what I carried in.
3. I will not damage living trees, shrubs or other natural features.
4. I will respect other people's property and rights.
5. I will lend a helping hand when I see someone in distress.
6. I will make myself and my snowmobile available to assist in search and rescue operations.
7. I will not interfere with or harass hikers, skiers, snowshoers, people who are ice fishing or participating in other winter sports. I will respect their rights to enjoy recreation facilities.
8. I will know and obey all federal, provincial and local rules regulating the operation of snowmobiles in areas where I use my snowmobile.
9. I will not harass wildlife. I will avoid areas posted for the protection of wildlife.
10. I will not snowmobile where snowmobiles are prohibited.

Chapter 1 — Summary

By the end of this section you should know:

- The licensing requirements to operate a snowmobile on roads and trails
- The importance of checking your snowmobile, preparing for trips and wearing proper protective gear
- Where you can and cannot drive your snowmobile
- The dangers of alcohol and driving on frozen lakes and rivers
- Hand signals, trails signs and traffic signs of specific to snowmobiles

Chapter 2

DRIVING AN OFF-ROAD VEHICLE

Off-road vehicles (sometimes called ORVs) are any two or three-wheeled motorized vehicles, as well as specific vehicles with four or more wheels as prescribed by regulation, intended for recreational use. Examples of off-road vehicles include all-terrain vehicles (ATVs), two-up ATVs, side-by-side ATVs, utility terrain vehicles (UTVs), amphibious ATVs, off-road motorcycles and dune buggies.

Note: Electric and motorized scooters (commonly known as go-peds) and pocket bikes (which are miniature motorcycles about two feet in height and with a speed of 70-80 km/h) are not off-road vehicles and, as such, cannot be registered as off-road vehicles. These vehicles also do not comply with motorcycle standards and cannot be registered as motorcycles.

I. Getting ready to drive an off-road vehicle

What you need to drive an off-road vehicle in Ontario

You must be 12 years of age or older to drive an off-road vehicle except on land occupied by the vehicle owner or under the close supervision of an adult. Direct and close supervision by an adult is recommended.

While off-road vehicles are generally not allowed on public roads, there are some exceptions. (See the section "Where you can and cannot drive.")

Registering and insuring your off-road vehicle

Off-road vehicles must be registered with the Ministry of Transportation at a Driver and Vehicle Licence Issuing Office. This applies to both new and used vehicles. You must be 16 years or older to register an off-road vehicle and you must be able to prove you own the vehicle.

If you buy a new off-road vehicle, you must get a certificate of sale from the dealer.

If you buy or transfer ownership of a used off-road vehicle, you must present the signed vehicle portion of the vehicle permit from the previous owner.

You must pay a fee to register your off-road vehicle. After registering, you will be given a vehicle permit and licence plate. You should carry the vehicle permit at all times unless you are operating the vehicle on land occupied by the owner of the vehicle.

If you have a two or three-wheeled vehicle, attach the licence plate to the front of the vehicle in plain view. If you have a vehicle with four or more wheels, attach the licence plate to the rear of the vehicle.

You must register your vehicle within six days of becoming the owner. If you change your address, you must notify the Ministry of Transportation within six days of the change. You may do this in person at a Driver and Vehicle Licence Issuing Office, ServiceOntario Kiosk, by mail to the Ministry of Transportation, P.O. Box 9200, Kingston, ON, K7L 5K4, or on the ServiceOntario website at www.serviceontario.ca.

If you are driving your off-road vehicle anywhere other than on the vehicle owner's property, you must also have vehicle liability insurance. You must carry the insurance card with you and show it if requested by a police officer. If someone else uses your off-road vehicle with your consent, you are both responsible for any penalties, damages or injuries that may occur.

The following vehicles do not need to be registered as off-road vehicles: road-building machines, farm vehicles, golf carts and motorized wheelchairs. In addition, off-road vehicles participating in a rally or competition sponsored by a motorcycle association with more than 25 members do not need to be registered for the event.

Wear a helmet

You must wear a motorcycle helmet, as required by the Highway Traffic Act, whenever you drive or ride on an off-road vehicle or on any vehicle towed by an off-road vehicle. The only exception is when you operate the vehicle on the property of the vehicle owner. The helmet must meet the standards approved for motorcycle helmets, or motor-assisted vehicle helmets, and must be fastened properly under the chin.

Protect your face and body

Always wear a face shield or goggles. A face shield can help prevent windburn, sunblindness and watering eyes from the wind. It can also protect your eyes from branches and twigs when driving through wooded areas. Wear pants that cover your legs, a long-sleeved shirt or jacket to protect your arms and gloves. Boots should be high enough to cover your ankles. To make yourself more visible to others while driving, wear brightly coloured clothing.

Make sure your vehicle is in good condition

Before every trip, check your vehicle to make sure it is in good working order. Your life may depend upon it. Check the vehicle thoroughly before you start to drive, including the following:

- Check the brake control to make sure it moves freely. Adjust if necessary.
- Check that the throttle opens and closes smoothly in all steering positions.
- Check the condition of the tires and tire pressure.

- Check the fuel lines and connections to make sure there are no leaks.
- Check that you have enough fuel and oil.
- Check that the engine is running smoothly. Make sure the vehicle is in neutral before starting the engine.
- Check that your lights are in good working condition.

Before you drive anywhere, read the owner's manual.

Be well prepared for every trip

Carefully preparing for every trip is an important safety measure. Check local weather forecasts and make sure you tell someone where you will be travelling and when you expect to be back. Use the buddy system; drive with others, not alone. Take along a first aid kit, a vehicle repair kit, an extra ignition key, a drive belt, spark plugs and a rope. On long trips, include a map and a compass (or a GPS unit and know how to use it), flashlight, hunting knife, hatchet, extra fuel and matches in a waterproof box.

II. Safe and responsible off-road vehicle driving

Where you can and cannot drive

You may not drive an off-road vehicle on most public roads in Ontario. This includes the area between the boundary or property lines, including medians, shoulders and ditches.

There are some exceptions:

- You may drive an off-road vehicle directly across some public roads.
- You may drive certain off-road vehicles with three or more wheels along some public roads when using the vehicle for farming or for licensed hunting or for the trapping of fur-bearing animals, provided that the vehicle weighs 450 kilograms or less and does not have an overall width greater than 1.35 metres (excluding mirrors).
- You may drive an off-road vehicle within a provincial or public park if it is permitted by the park authority.
- Emergency personnel, such as police officers and firefighters, who are performing necessary duties in the course of their work or who are responding to an emergency, may drive off-road vehicles on public roads.

There are also exceptions for the category of off-road vehicles known as all-terrain vehicles (ATVs).

If you do drive an off-road vehicle on or across a public road, you must be at least 16 years of age and have a valid Ontario driver's licence (Class G2, M2 or higher).

You may not operate an off-road vehicle in such a way as to disrupt or destroy the natural environment including fish habitats, property and plants or trees.

For more specific information on where you may operate off-road vehicles, and what rules you must follow when doing so, you should refer to the Highway Traffic Act and the Off-Road Vehicles Act.

All-terrain vehicles (ATVs)

All-terrain vehicles (ATVs) are off-road vehicles with the following characteristics: four wheels, all of which are in contact with the ground; steering handlebars; and a seat designed to be straddled by the driver.

There are sections of provincial highways in Ontario where you may drive an ATV on the shoulder provided the ATV weighs 450 kilograms or less, does not have an overall width greater than 1.35 metres (excluding mirrors), meets the requirements of the federal Motor Vehicle Safety Act (MVSA) and the American National Standards Institute (ANSI) Standard, and is designed to carry only a driver and no passengers. You must travel in the same direction as the traffic using that side of the road. If there is no shoulder, if the shoulder is obstructed or if you are crossing a level railway crossing, you may drive your vehicle on the paved part of the highway. Keep as close as safely possible to the right of the shoulder or edge of the highway as you can.

Where a road or highway falls under the authority of a municipality, the municipality must enact a by-law for ATVs to be allowed access to the road. If there is no by-law in place, you cannot drive an ATV on that road. The municipality may also pass by-laws to decide where and when ATVs may be used on these local roads.

For those roads and highways where you are permitted to drive an ATV, you must obey all licensing and operational requirements, and your vehicle must conform to all equipment requirements, as listed in the Highway Traffic Act and the Off-Road Vehicles Act. Remember the following rules:

1. You must have a valid Ontario driver's licence (G2, M2 or higher).
2. You must wear a motorcycle helmet with a chin strap that is securely fastened.
3. You cannot carry passengers on your vehicle.
4. You must drive at speed limits lower than those posted: where the posted speed is 50km/h or less, you must drive 20 km/h or less; where the posted speed is over 50 km/h, you must drive 50 km/h or less.

In general, ATVs are not permitted on controlled access highways, such as the 400 series highways and most parts of the Trans-Canada highway, but are allowed access to highways 500 to 899, the 7000 series highways and highways with low traffic volumes.

For more details about which highways ATVs may drive on, please refer to the Highway Traffic Act, Ontario Regulation 316/03.

Obey the rules

You must stop if a police officer signals you to do so. You can also be stopped by a landowner when you are driving on private property. If signalled to stop by an authorized person, you must stop and, if asked, properly identify yourself.

Everyone who drives an off-road vehicle without care and attention or without reasonable consideration for other people and property may be charged with careless driving. Other offences, such as dangerous driving and alcohol related offences, apply to drivers of off-road vehicles. When you drive an off-road vehicle on a public road, the Highway Traffic Act offences also apply.

Report collisions to the police

You must report to the police immediately any collision on a public highway that results in injury to any person or damage to property apparently exceeding $1000.

Do not drink and drive

It is against the law to drive an off-road vehicle when you are impaired by alcohol or drugs.

Drinking and driving is a deadly combination.

Consuming any amount of alcohol before you ride affects your ability to make good decisions. Even one drink can reduce your ability to concentrate and react to things that happen suddenly when you are driving. With more alcohol in your blood, you could have trouble judging distances and your vision may become blurred. Factors like tiredness, your mood, and how long ago you ate and how much, can make a difference in how alcohol affects your driving ability.

The police can stop any driver to determine if alcohol or drug testing is required. They may also do roadside spot checks. When stopped by the police, you may be told to blow into a machine that tests your breath for alcohol, a roadside screening device, or perform physical co-ordination tests. If you fail or refuse to provide a breath sample or to perform the physical co-ordination tests, you will be charged under the *Criminal Code*.

If the reading on the machine shows you have been drinking, you may be taken to a police station for a breathalyzer test. The breathalyzer uses your breath to measure the amount of alcohol in your bloodstream.

If you cannot give a breath sample or it is impracticable to obtain a sample of breath, the police officer can require you to provide a blood sample instead.

If the police believe that a driver is impaired because of the consumption of a drug or a combination of alcohol and a drug, the police can also require a driver to submit to an evaluation and then require a driver to provide blood, oral fluid or urine samples. If you fail or refuse to comply with any of these demands, you will be charged under the *Criminal Code.*

Driving impaired or with more than 80 milligrams of alcohol in 100 millilitres of blood (.08) is an offence under the *Criminal Code.* Even if your blood alcohol concentration is less than .08, you can still be charged with impaired driving under the *Criminal Code.*

You will receive an immediate 90-day Administrative Driver's Licence Suspension if your blood alcohol concentration (BAC) is more than .08 or if you fail or refuse to provide a breath or bodily fluid sample, perform a physical co-ordination test or submit to an evaluation.

If you register in the "warn range" of .05 to .08 on a roadside screening device, you will receive an immediate driver's licence suspension. For a first occurrence, you will be suspended for 3 days. For a second occurrence in a five-year period, you will be immediately suspended for 7 days and you must undergo a remedial alcohol education program. For a third or subsequent time in a five-year period, you will be immediately suspended for 30 days and you must undergo a remedial alcohol treatment program and have an ignition interlock condition placed on your licence for 6 months. If you choose not to install an ignition interlock device, you must not drive until the condition is removed from your licence.

If you are 21 years old and under and hold a full class driver's licence you must not drive if you have been drinking alcohol. Your blood alcohol level must be zero. If you are caught driving with alcohol in your blood, you will receive an immediate driver's licence suspension at the roadside for 24 hours and, if convicted, you will face a fine of $60–$500 and a 30-day licence suspension.

Drivers of all ages in either Level One or Level Two of Ontario's graduated licensing system must also have a blood alcohol level of zero when driving. New drivers caught drinking and driving will receive an immediate driver's licence suspension at the roadside for 24 hours and, if convicted, will face a fine of $60–$500 and will receive a suspension period as per the Novice

Driver Escalating Sanctions scheme. For the first occurrence, you will be suspended for 30 days. For the second occurrence, in a five-year period, you be suspended for 90 days. For the third occurrence in a five-year period, the novice portion of your driver's licence will be cancelled and you must reapply for a G1 licence.

Novice drivers will also be charged under the *Criminal Code* if their BAC exceeds .08 and will be issued a "warn range" suspension if they register a BAC from .05 to .08.

Drugs

Any drug that changes your mood or the way you see and feel about the world around you will affect the way you drive. *Criminal Code* and HTA sanctions apply to drivers impaired by alcohol or a drug.

In circumstances involving possible impairment by a drugs or a combination of alcohol and a drug, police can require a driver to perform physical co-ordination tests and to submit to an evaluation and then require a driver to provide blood, oral fluid or urine samples. If you fail or refuse to comply with any of these demands, you will be charged under the *Criminal Code*. You will also receive an immediate 90-day Administrative Driver's Licence Suspension.

Illegal drugs such as marijuana and cocaine are not the only problem. Some drugs that your doctor may prescribe for you and some over-the-counter drugs can also impair your driving. Here are some points you should remember:

- If you use prescription medicines or get allergy shots, ask your doctor about side effects such as dizziness, blurred vision, nausea or drowsiness that could affect your driving.
- Read the information on the package of any over-the-counter medicine you take. Any stimulant, diet pill, tranquillizer or sedative may affect your driving. Even allergy and cold remedies may have ingredients that could affect your driving.
- Drugs and any amount of alcohol together can have dangerous effects, even several days after you have taken the drug. Do not take a chance, ask your doctor or pharmacist.

Do not carry passengers

Do not carry passengers on an off-road vehicle designed for one person. Carrying passengers changes the weight distribution of the vehicle and limits your ability to shift position on the vehicle for control and stability.

Practice safe driving skills

Driving an off-road vehicle is different than driving any other type of vehicle and takes more skill than you might think. Be sure to read your owner's manual before you begin to drive.

If you are a beginner, practice driving your vehicle in an open area that is free of obstacles, until you become skilled at handling it. Choose ground that is uniform, either dirt, sand or snow. Avoid paved surfaces when driving an off-road vehicle. Off-road vehicles are designed for off-road use and are more difficult to manoeuvre on paved surfaces. When driving, keep both feet on the footrests at all times. Do not try to stabilize a tipping vehicle by putting your foot down. You could run over your foot or leg.

Be extremely careful driving through water. Driving fast across unknown water is dangerous. Hidden rocks or holes could throw you off the vehicle and cause serious injury or drowning. First, check that the water is not too deep. Drive slowly and carefully so you can steer around rocks and other obstacles.

Always use a flag mast when driving in dunes and hills. Remember that you need a running start to climb most hills. Be extra cautious when driving among pedestrians, horseback riders, sunbathers or bicyclists.

Read the Snowmobiler's Code of Ethics (page 194) and follow it when driving your off-road vehicle.

Chapter 2 — Summary

By the end of this section you should know:

- The licensing requirements to operate an off-road vehicle on roads and trails
- The importance of checking your off-road vehicle, preparing for trips and wearing proper protective gear
- Where you can and cannot drive your off-road vehicle
- The dangers of alcohol and driving an off-road vehicle

Index — Part One: The Official Driver's Handbook

Index — Part Two: Off-Road Vehicles

NOW THERE ARE MORE WAYS THAN EVER TO EXPRESS YOURSELF!

Personalize your licence plates — with two to eight characters, as well as a great choice of colour graphics. Then you'll really stand out from the crowd.

Turn the page to find out more.

Other MTO Publications for you

Copies of this handbook and others may be purchased from a:

- **Retail store near you;**
- **DriveTest Centre;**
- **Driver and Vehicle Licence Issuing Office; or**
- **By calling (416) 326-5300 or 1-800-668-9938 (toll free)**
- **www.serviceontario.ca/publications**

Prepayment required by credit card – VISA or Mastercard.
You may also pay with a certified cheque, bank draft or money order at DriveTest Centres.

Online versions of the Official MTO Handbooks can be viewed (Read Only) on the MTO Website via the following links:

English: http://www.mto.gov.on.ca/english/pubs/drivhand/index.shtml
French: http://www.mto.gov.on.ca/french/pubs/drivhand/index.shtml

Handbook prices are subject to 5% H.S.T and 5% shipping costs. The road map is subject to 13% H.S.T., and 5% shipping costs.

- The Official Driver's Handbook
- The Official Motorcycle Handbook
- The Official Truck Handbook
- The Official Bus Handbook
- The Official Air Brake Handbook
- The Official Ontario Road Map